THE SUPERNATURAL POWER OF
DELIVERANCE

Experiencing the Power of the Blood of Jesus to Set the Captive Free

MELINDA LAGAAY

Copyright © 2023
MELINDA LAGAAY
THE SUPERNATURAL POWER OF DELIVERANCE
Experiencing the Power of the Blood of Jesus to Set the Captive Free
All rights reserved.

No part of this publication may be reproduced, distributed, or transmitted in any form or by any means, including photocopying, recording, or other electronic or mechanical methods, without the prior written permission of the author, except in the case of brief quotations embodied in critical reviews and certain other non-commercial uses permitted by copyright law.

MELINDA LAGAAY

Printed in the United States.
First Printing 2023
First Edition 2023

Paperback ISBN: 978-1-7378073-1-5

10 9 8 7 6 5 4 3 2 1

Edited by Angela Parker
Cover Design by Zoltan Hercik
Arise and Shine Ministries www.ariseandshinetoday.com

Scriptures marked NIV are taken from the NEW INTERNATIONAL VERSION (NIV): Scripture taken from THE HOLY BIBLE, NEW INTERNATIONAL VERSION ®. Copyright© 1973, 1978, 1984, 2011 by Biblica, Inc.TM. Used by permission of Zondervan.
Scriptures marked NKJV are taken from the NEW KING JAMES VERSION (NKJV): Scripture taken from the NEW KING JAMES VERSION®. Copyright© 1982 by Thomas Nelson, Inc. Used by permission. All rights reserved.
Scriptures marked TPT are from The Passion Translation®. Copyright © 2017, 2018, 2020 by Passion & Fire Ministries, Inc. Used by permission. All rights reserved. ThePassionTranslation.com.
Scripture taken from the Amplified Bible (AMPCE), Copyright © 1954, 1958, 1962, 1964, 1965, 1987 by The Lockman Foundation. Used by permission.
Scripture quotations marked (AMPCE) are taken from the Amplified Bible, Copyright © 1954, 1958, 1962, 1964, 1965, 1987 by The Lockman Foundation. Used by permission.
Scripture taken from the Amplified Bible, Copyright © 2015 by The Lockman Foundation. Used by permission.
Scripture quotations marked (AMP) are taken from the Amplified Bible, Copyright © 2015 by The Lockman Foundation. Used by permission.
Scripture quotations are from The ESV® Bible (The Holy Bible, English Standard Version®), © 2001 by Crossway, a publishing ministry of Good News Publishers. Used by permission. All rights reserved.

THE SUPERNATURAL POWER OF
DELIVERANCE

Dedication

I dedicate this book first to my husband Pieter. Your journey into freedom and your heart to see others set free inspires me daily. I am so proud of you. I love you! Lastly, my amazing children, Sander, Kaitlyn, and Ava. I am so proud of you. Your love and support has been one of my greatest motivations.

Acknowledgments

I thank my friends and family who made this book possible.

My Mom, LaDonna, and her husband, Phil, for their consistent love, home cooked meals, and endless support.

My Dad, Geoff, who is in heaven cheering me on. Thank you for years of support and love while you were here.

My sister, Lisa, who is my best friend and whose passion for Jesus inspires me daily. My brother and sister, Isabella and Jeffrey, and his fiance Bianca. I am so grateful for you in my life.

Steve and Wendy Backlund, for believing in me when I needed it the most. Thank you for your mentorship and support. Thank you for teaching Pieter and me how to think and believe like Jesus.

My friend and former Bethel School of Supernatural Ministry Mentor, Angela Parker, for hours and hours of editing, endless support, laughs, love, and coffee.

Ash Anderson, Connie Jones, and the entire Igniting Hope team, for your friendship, support, and leadership.

Jeanne Dillion, at Transforming Hearts Ministries, for leading our marriage into freedom and teaching us how to love with our whole heart.

Francesco Sideli, for believing in our marriage and teaching us about freedom through inner healing and deliverance.

Lastly, thank you to Bethel, my church home. I am eternally grateful to be a part of this passionate church community. I will cherish my time in this house of God forever.

Endorsements

There are few people I admire more than Melinda Lagaay, and her book The Supernatural Power of Deliverance captures her unique anointing of wisdom, power, love, and hope. Melinda and her husband, Pieter, have greatly and positively impacted Igniting Hope Ministries and I'm fully convinced their testimony will impact you. I highly recommend this book to you.

- Steve Backlund, Co-Founder of Igniting Hope Ministries

This powerful story of redemption, restoration, and reconciliation builds faith and brings hope into seemingly hopeless situations, laying out a pathway of practical spiritual tools that leads to true freedom. As senior pastors of Valley Church, with 30+ years of hands-on ministry experience, we highly endorse Melinda's book as a resource that sheds light on the reality and need for deliverance ministry within the context of marriage.

- Pastors Lynn & Renae Hardy, Valley Church, Caldwell Idaho

Table of Contents

Foreword 1
Introduction 3
SECTION ONE 5
    The Supernatural Power of Deliverance
Chapter 1 7
    My Story
Chapter 2 15
    Deliverance from Demons
Chapter 3 29
    The Believer's Authority
Chapter 4 47
    Healing the Wounded Soul
Chapter 5 63
    Tearing Down Strongholds in the Mind
SECTION TWO 73
    Supernatural Prayers for Deliverance
Chapter 6 75
    Breaking Generational Curses - The Power of a Blessing
Chapter 7 83
    The Power of Forgiveness
Chapter 8 97
    Overcoming Pride - by Pieter Lagaay
Chapter 9 107
    Redeeming Purity and Sex in Marriage - by Pieter Lagaay
Chapter 10 115
    Breaking Free from Witchcraft and the Occult
Chapter 11 125
    Freedom from Hypocrisy
Chapter 12 129
    Worshiping Idols
Chapter 13 133
    Freedom from Rebellion
Chapter 14 137
    Arise and Shine Ministries Deliverance Model
Chapter 15 147
    Follow up Care for Deliverance

FOREWORD

If you love Jesus, but can't seem to walk the walk, this book is for you. In this book Melinda shares that our sin is not the problem, sin is our unhealthy solution to our real problem. Too many people have focused on the sin rather than the problem that drives us to sin.

I highly recommend this book for those who have tried and failed and are ready to give up. This book is for those living under guilt and shame and need hope. And perhaps most of all for those who inwardly know they are not experiencing the freedom and the joy-filled life that Jesus promised.

Melinda shares her journey into freedom in a way that not only brings hope but some practical guides to freedom. She and her husband, Pieter have overcome much and are now walking in authority and wisdom to help others.

I know Melinda personally and can honestly say that I admire not only her love for God, but her passion to see others set free to live the abundant life Jesus promised. She is a woman I wholly trust, and I believe she has an anointing and a call to heal the brokenhearted and set the captives free.

I pray that everyone who reads this book will be covered by the love of God and the supernatural strength of God to become overcomers like Melinda.

Wendy Backlund, Co-Founder of Igniting Hope Ministries

Introduction

"How God anointed Jesus of Nazareth with the Holy Spirit and with power, who went about doing good and healing all who were oppressed by the devil, for God was with Him." Acts 10:38 NKJV

Demons are real, and they can oppress believers. I know this because years ago, I was the one who was bound. I was a born-again, Spirit-filled Christian, yet I was not living in full freedom. Looking at me, you would never have known that I was struggling because I looked great on the outside. I lived a comfortable life with my husband and three children, and we appeared to "have it all together." My husband was a doctor, and I was a stay-at-home mom. But the truth was we were both oppressed, and we needed the blood of Jesus and the power of the Holy Spirit to set us free. Christians cannot be possessed, because they are the possession of Christ, but they can be oppressed. In this book I explain the difference and tell the story of how Jesus set me free.

I have learned that the battle for our freedom is spiritual, and it must be fought spiritually. Paul said in Ephesians 6 that, "we do not wrestle against flesh and blood, but against principalities, against powers, against the rulers of the darkness of this age, against spiritual hosts of wickedness in the heavenly places." This scripture is not a metaphor, rather a reality.

Jesus walked around casting out demons and healing all who the devil oppressed, and believers are called to do the same. The good news is the blood of Jesus paid for our freedom - not partial freedom, but complete freedom. But without the knowledge that we are in a spiritual battle, we will continue to see born-again believers who are burned out, weary, and who want to give up. We need the real resurrection power of the blood of Jesus and the power of the Holy Spirit to set us free. "And you know that

God anointed Jesus of Nazareth with the Holy Spirit and with power. Then Jesus went around doing good and healing all who were oppressed by the devil, for God was with him." Acts 10:38 NLT.

I wrote this book for people like me who know there is more to the Christian life than "just getting by." I am here to tell you that complete freedom is possible. The blood of Jesus contains the power to set you free from anything you are facing, whether your struggle is with anxiety, depression, fear, suicidal thoughts, anger, rage, confusion, rejection, or heaviness. This book will equip you to find freedom for yourself and equip you to go out and set the captives free.

I was once captive, but Jesus set me free! As you read this book, I pray you find hope, freedom, and joy in its pages. You are not alone on your journey to freedom. Your story will become a powerful testimony that will give others the courage to believe that true transformation is possible with Jesus.

"...For the testimony of Jesus is the spirit of prophecy." Revelation 19:10 NKJV

SECTION ONE

The Supernatural Power of Deliverance

Chapter 1

My Story

"He heals the brokenhearted And binds up their wounds."

Psalms 147:3 NKJV

Many years ago, my marriage was falling apart. It was during this season that I discovered the truth of my husband's addiction to pornography and his involvement in affairs. Six years of marriage crumbled beneath the weight of this devastating news. The truth of his sex and pornography addiction was exposed on a family vacation in Lake Tahoe. A text message on Pieter's phone uncovered the painful reality. Our lives were forever altered in a single moment. I was crushed, devastated, and heartbroken, to say the least.

The night everything came out was painful. We stayed up that night crying and talking until I could not talk anymore. There was simply nothing left to say. I was crushed and devastated. I was imagining the worst-case scenario for how this would all play out. My heart was hurting for our children, who would eventually hear the news. What was I going to do? What would Pieter do? Pieter didn't want a divorce, but how could I stay? My mind was spinning as I thought about the future and what it could look like without Pieter in it.

By 1 am I was completely exhausted. Pieter and I had a long and painful conversation, and by the end of the night, there was nothing left to say. We finally fell asleep, and something supernatural happened around 2 am. Pieter found himself kneeling by the bed, feeling overwhelmed with a sense of hopelessness. Deep inside, he hated who he had become.

Whispering, "I can't fix this" he turned to look at a mirror on the dresser, and a vision unfolded before him. He was taken to a valley, where he found himself on his hands and knees, face buried in the dirt. At that moment, he felt a firm grasp on the back of his neck, and as he looked up, he saw the hand of Jesus reaching out to him. Standing face to face with Jesus, Pieter's gaze shifted to a long road winding through a valley, ascending rolling hills, and leading to a mountain range.

As Pieter surveyed the long road he knew the road was for him. He knew it was a road meant for longevity and perseverance. The words Jesus spoke to Pieter were simple, "Walk with me on this path. It's not a race, just a walk. I will always be on this path with you no matter where you go." All Pieter said was "ok." The vision ended and Pieter knew that his freedom would have to go through the surrender to Jesus. At the same time, I heard an audible voice say, "I am going to restore your marriage!" The word "encounter" in the "Jesus" sense was not even in our vocabulary. Pieter was not yet a believer, and although I was a Christian, I had no idea God could take you into a vision or speak to you audibly.

When we woke up in the morning, Pieter told me about his vision and I told him about the voice I heard. I was shocked, and so was Pieter. I had no idea how I would move past the pain of infidelity, but I knew if God was with us, I was willing to try. Pieter gave his life to Jesus that very moment, and I knew the prayers I had written in my journal were being fulfilled. We were in a pit and by His grace and mercy, He was rescuing us.

I had been praying for years for our marriage, even though I had no idea what to pray for. One day I was praying and wrote in my journal, "Jesus, do whatever it takes to bring Pieter to you." This is one of those prayers I knew could cost a great deal, but I also knew the reward of Pieter being saved outweighed the cost. Of course, I was devastated and completely broken from what I had learned Pieter was secretly doing, but I also had a small amount of hope (the belief that things could change), and sometimes that's all God needs to do a mighty work. The Bible tells us if we have faith as small as a mustard seed we can move mountains, and we certainly had a big mountain in front of us (see Matthew 17:20).

On the drive home, Pieter and I started the process of talking about the next steps to try to restore what was left of our marriage. I knew we needed a church, so we decided to start attending our local congregation. Pieter was determined to pursue healing, so he signed up for counseling, individual and group therapy, and a men's group. For the next three years, we pursued putting our marriage back together. We traveled around the country to what I call "Jesus" conferences. We would go to altar calls, and get prayer, over and over again. I kept asking God to send an angel to "zap" us and make us feel better. I asked the Lord one day, "Is ' survival mode' really as good as it gets?" The Bible says that the Kingdom of God is "Righteousness, peace, and joy in the Holy Spirit (see Romans 14:17)"; if that was the case, we were experiencing a very small portion of the Kingdom.

My life living up to the moment in Lake Tahoe where I discovered what Pieter was doing was emotionally exhausting. My Dad was diagnosed with cancer. He moved in with us and passed away three weeks later. My Mom had gone through a divorce after being married for over twenty years. I felt the burden of the family on my shoulders, but it was during this season that my hunger for God was growing. I just wanted Jesus. When the kids were at school I would spend hours in prayer, seeking God, listening to sermons and worship music, reading the Bible, and just soaking in God's presence. I wanted to know Him, and I knew that He had what I needed to be set free from the pain in my heart and the anxiety I was experiencing.

My dream life exploded in this season and God began to speak to me about the future through dreams in the night. One night during the covid lockdown I had a dream that I was at Bethel Church in Redding, California. I was at the front of the sanctuary and there was a large red chair at the front of the sanctuary sitting next to me. I heard a voice say, "That seat is for you!" I could see many of the pastors and leaders in the dream and the auditorium was filled with people. I was not wearing a shirt in the dream, but I was not embarrassed. I sat down in the red chair and woke up from the dream. I immediately wrote every detail of the dream in my journal. "What could this mean?", I wondered. I prayed and asked the Lord for an interpretation. I also called the only person I knew who could interpret dreams. My friend told me, "You have a seat at Bethel! You're supposed to go to Redding!" I responded, "We can't move to Redding. That's crazy! I don't know how that could ever happen." But something inside of me came alive when she said it, and a seed was planted. Deep down at that moment, I knew we were supposed to move to Redding.

Three weeks earlier, my sister Lisa had a dream and saw me standing in a Spanish style house in the country, surrounded by oak trees. She described the house in detail, down to the arched doorways and the Spanish style flooring. I was standing in one of the rooms of the house, and while I was standing there, the doors blew open behind me and leaves started blowing all around me. Lisa said, "The leaves represent healing for the nations." I wrote the dream down and felt like Mary who "pondered all of these things in her heart." (see Luke 2:19) "What could all of this mean?", I wondered once more.

"In the middle of its street, and on either side of the river, was the tree of life, which bore twelve fruits, each tree yielding its fruit every month. The leaves of the tree were for the healing of the nations." Revelation 22:2 NKJV

Fortunately, Pieter and I were home a lot during the pandemic, which gave us time to discuss our future. I told him about my dream and the one Lisa had. "I think God is telling us we should move to Redding," I said, "and that I should attend ministry school there." We prayed and agreed to drive up to Redding the following weekend to check it out, despite the pandemic.

My mom LaDonna and I drove up to Redding to look at houses with Pieter. He wanted to rent a place and keep our Bay Area home, but I felt we should sell and fully move. We compromised to look at rentals and homes for sale. I found a listing for a perfect home on seven acres with a pool and made an appointment.

The next day, I went to see the house with my mom while Pieter worked. On the way, I texted the listing to my sister Lisa. As we toured the property, Lisa called me shocked. "Melinda, this is the house from my dream!" I had forgotten her dream's details. At that moment, I knew - God wanted us to move here. This was meant to be our new home. I walked through the house stunned. The room Lisa saw me in was there - Spanish tiled floors, arched doors, just as she'd described.

"And it shall come to pass in the last days, says God, That I will pour out of My Spirit on all flesh; Your sons and your daughters shall prophesy, Your young men shall see visions, Your old men shall dream dreams." Acts 2:17 NKJV

The problem was, we had nothing to offer to buy the new home. Our home in the bay area was almost paid off completely, so we could pay cash for the home, but our home was not for sale and it needed work. Bottom line - we had nothing to offer the owners except, "Please wait for us to sell our home, so that we can buy your home eventually." But something inside of me just knew we were getting the house. My Mom and I left the house that day, and I called Pieter and told him I found the house we were supposed to buy. He was hesitant and wanted to see the property for himself. He also wanted to look at other properties, which I agreed to do, despite knowing deep down that this was the home for us.

We drove to the home the following day and I was praying the whole time that Pieter would see this home as a blessing from God. Pieter walked around the property and was very quiet as he surveyed the land. Inside I was bursting, because I thought to myself and knew, THIS is our HOME! After looking at the house, I agreed to view other properties in the area. Every other house we visited was not a fit, and I knew why. We already had a home!

Pieter finally agreed to make an offer on the Spanish style home that was surrounded by oak trees. We called the realtor and told him the news. The realtor wrote up the full-price offer and presented it to the owners. Finally, the call from the realtor came. The owners rejected our offer. Actually, this was the right thing for them to do. We were asking them to wait for us to list and sell our home in the Bay Area. I would have rejected that kind of offer too! But I just knew we were getting the house.

I told Pieter, let's go home and call a realtor and get our Bay Area home ready to sell in faith. That is what we did. We came back to the Bay Area and started getting our home ready to sell, which was not easy during the covid pandemic, but God. God had a plan for us, and I just knew that nothing was going to stop what God wanted to do.

Three days later the realtor called us and said, "The owners have decided to accept your offer." We were ecstatic! The owners gave us 30 days to have an offer in our hands, so we began feverishly painting, and adding new flooring throughout the house.

After deciding to move to Redding, it felt like everything started breaking in our house. First, the oven stopped working. Then the fridge sprang a leak, flooding the wood floors. At the same time, a laundry room leak ruined more flooring. It was like chaos erupted once we agreed to the move! In hindsight, these trials only strengthened my resilience and conviction. Each new appliance failure or water damage issue further confirmed we had made the right choice. It was as if the enemy wanted to thwart our plans, so he unleashed mayhem. But I remained steadfast in faith through each setback. Cleaning up the mess and making repairs, I felt assured of our decision more than ever.

"My brethren, count it all joy when you fall into various trials, knowing that the testing of your faith produces patience. But let patience have its perfect work, that you may be perfect and complete, lacking nothing." James 1:2-4 NKJV

A key factor in moving was Pieter getting a job, which he insisted on. Miraculously, he was offered one in Chico, an hour's drive from Redding. Though amazing, I felt unsure in my spirit this was God's plan. I started sensing Pieter and I were supposed to attend ministry school together. I brought up the idea, but he was fully convinced he was supposed to work. Pieter had recently graduated from law school, so he was seeking employment at a law firm. Meanwhile, I was fully convinced that Pieter was supposed to take a break and come to ministry school with me.

"A man's heart plans his way, But the Lord directs his steps." Proverbs 16:9 NKJV

While preparing to move, Pieter began his new remote job. Miraculously, our home sold in under 24 hours! However, just days before our move to Redding, he was let go - as the most recent hire, he was first to be cut due to pandemic downsizing. Pieter called to tell me the news, but I knew God was at work. This was clearing the path for Pieter to join me in ministry school, though he still felt unsure. Exactly 45 days after first visiting Redding, we officially moved into our new home!

I'll never forget after the movers left, collapsing amid boxes in our new bedroom, tears falling as I stared at the ceiling. After pretending for years that our brokenness was wholeness, God's call to move here felt like a lifeline. Alone on the carpet, I let waves of pent-up pain, trauma and disappointment wash over me. Our seemingly picture-perfect life had been one big lie. I was exhausted and broken, desperately needing healing. But finally moving here sparked hope that our future could be different.

Through tears, all I could pray was, "Thank you, Jesus, for bringing us here." I didn't know what awaited at ministry school, I only knew for certain that God had good plans for our family. The past held such hurt, yet here I sensed the dawn of something better. A chance to be free from lies and find healing. Alone in the empty bedroom, my heart overflowed with gratitude. This move was the start of a journey back to life, one step at a time with Jesus. The boxes surrounding me were just the shell - God was reshaping us from the inside out, into who we were truly meant to be all along.

"The righteous cry out, and the Lord hears, and delivers them out of all of their troubles. The Lord is near to those who have a broken heart, And saves such as have a contrite spirit." Psalm 34:17-18 NKJV

Chapter 2

Deliverance from Demons

"Anything hidden is a playground for the enemy."

Pieter & Melinda Lagaay

Pieter and I loved playing tennis, so when we moved to Redding, joining the local tennis club was one of the first things we did. As summer was winding down, Pieter was out playing with some other club members one day. One of the men asked if Pieter had moved to Redding to attend ministry school. I could not shake the feeling that Pieter was supposed to attend ministry school with me. I had told Pieter I thought he was supposed to join me at school, but ultimately I decided to leave the issue alone and let God speak to his heart. Pieter felt stirred in his heart when the man asked this question - I was completely unaware that Pieter had been wrestling with God for months about going to ministry school with me.

Pieter had been applying for jobs all summer. Despite his persistent efforts, he was unable to get a single interview. Pieter came home from tennis that day and prayed to God on the drive home. He said, "God, I think I am supposed to go to ministry school. I am going to go home and talk to Melinda, but you have to stop me if you don't want me to go." Pieter heard nothing. This conversation with God continued all the way home. Pieter parked the car and walked into the house. With ministry school starting in two days, Pieter walked through the door and said to me, "I think I am supposed to go to ministry school with you." I ran to Pieter and gave him a big hug and said, "Let's contact the admissions counselor!"

Ministry School

Two days later, Pieter and I were standing together in the Redding Civic Auditorium for our first day of ministry school at Bethel Supernatural School of Ministry. I had come seeking God, but I was also desiring healing and personal transformation. I was exhausted, hurting, and broken. I can say that I was broken now, but when I started school I had no idea just how wounded my soul really was.

Sitting in ministry school was painful for me, although I hid those feelings from everyone. I wanted so much to encounter God, but not at the cost of being vulnerable in front of others. I had learned to put walls up around my heart to protect myself from being hurt. The walls of self-protection kept me with a feeling of security.

I would go home from school many days and cry. I would do anything to avoid crying at school. I had learned to hide my heart at a very young age because of the pain I had experienced during childhood. My parents were amazing, but my young heart did not know how to process a divorce. I learned to keep everyone happy by pretending to be happy all the time. I learned that hiding my heart protected me from experiencing pain. Of course, what I was really doing was storing up pain in my soul.

Living this way was extremely painful, but it made me feel safe. Anyone reading this who has tried fiercely to protect their heart from any pain knows what I am talking about. The real problem was - I was living in massive amounts of shame. Shame caused me to hide my heart from others. Shame says, "You will never be good enough." Brené Brown defines shame as "the intensely painful feeling or experience of believing that we are flawed and therefore unworthy of love and belonging."

Ultimately, I felt unworthy of receiving love. I wanted so desperately to encounter God during school, and everytime someone would share a testimony about encountering God's love, outwardly I would smile, but inside a voice would whisper, "You are unworthy of experiencing God's love because of your past." Of course, this was a major lie! But at the time it felt so real.

My wounded soul was covered in scars from the pain of my past.

But God in His kindness had a plan to heal my soul. I can say confidently now that although waiting on God is hard, God is faithful to answer our prayers at just the right time. I had prayed for years for God to "fix me." I had no idea what I really needed, but He knew, and He was setting me up. He was setting Pieter up too!

Ministry school was going great - until it wasn't. The problem was, we were trying to process and unpack a lifetime of pain, but we had no idea where to start. We decided to reach out to our revival group pastor for help. Later that week, we sat in a meeting with our pastor, telling him our entire life story. His response was, "You guys have never been delivered?" Pieter and I were shocked at his response to our story. I thought, "Isn't deliverance for crazy demon-possessed people?" We had no idea that the bondage we were in was spiritual and we were under the weight of demonic oppression.

We were what I like to call, "highly functioning demonically oppressed Christians." No one would have looked at us and assumed we "had" a demon. The idea was almost laughable. Pieter was a doctor and I was a stay-at-home mom. We both appeared to have it all together. I wasn't "hearing voices" yet, when our pastor explained our need for deliverance, something inside of me knew he was right. We needed freedom from the weight we were feeling and the pain we were experiencing.

Our pastor referred us to Transforming Hearts Ministries for inner healing, deliverance, and counseling with Jeanne Dillon. Our revival group pastor, Francesco, said something to us that changed our lives forever, *"Anything you hide will give power to the enemy."* Pieter and I agreed when we went into our session that everything would come out, no matter how vulnerable it was. Nothing could remain hidden if we wanted to be free.

The night before our first counseling session, Pieter and I prayed together and agreed to full transparency - no more hiding. I'd lived much of my life not knowing Jesus, so there were things pre-marriage I'd never shared, even vowing "I'll never tell anyone." Pieter had similar secret vows to keep buried his past mistakes and shame. But we learned vulnerability destroys shame and cultivates freedom. We committed to fully opening up in our sessions, "letting it all out" for healing.

Two weeks after meeting our pastor, we spent 6 intense, life-changing days in counselor Jeanne Dillon's office. What happened there transformed us forever. Years of suppressed pain, guilt and secrets came pouring out. The rawness was agonizing yet so freeing. What happened there changed our lives forever!

Freedom from Demonic Oppression

The first few days of our sessions with Jeanne were spent sharing our entire life story. Every - single - detail, came out. Even the things we said we would, "Take to the grave." Pieter went first. I sat and listened as Pieter shared the story of his childhood. I had heard some of his story before, but not the way I heard it in that office. I listened to him recounting the times he was alone as a little boy. His Mom (although she was an amazing Mom) would drink and sometimes forget to pick him up from school. He was often left alone in his room without anyone to care for his heart. All of the sudden things were making sense - Pieter never learned what real love looked like. He was still that same little boy sitting on his bed, looking to be loved. He wanted to have his heart cared for, and so he sought approval from anyone who would give him attention.

On day two, it was my turn to share my story. I was so nervous about sharing my heart, but I had promised Pieter to be vulnerable, so I let it all out. I shared the story of my childhood and how I learned to seek approval from others through my performance. Love was often validated to me when I did things well, or when I performed well enough. I grew up being the "perfect child." The oldest, and therefore, I was the example. I learned to receive love by performing well enough for my parents and for men. If I didn't measure up to the level of standard I had made for myself, I would experience shame and unworthiness. Although, I never would have called it shame at the time. I learned how to protect my heart at all costs to prevent myself from experiencing pain. I hid my heart from everyone.

I discovered that the key to unlocking my heart was in processing my life story. This step is so important because the motivation of our hearts is often the foundation we are standing on - which in my case, was shame and unworthiness. Ministry school tackled my feelings of shame and unworthiness head-on. The first year was focused entirely on our identity in Christ. But because my identity was rooted in performance, I had learned to receive God's love by being "good enough." But, God was setting me up. He wanted to teach me how to be a daughter. He wanted me to stand on the foundation of His perfect love and approval of me, regardless of what I did to earn it. The truth is, the Father loves us just as we are. There is nothing we can do to earn His love - it is received entirely by grace. His love is a gift. The shame and unworthiness I was carrying around had to go. I needed an encounter with the Father's perfect love, and I was about to have an encounter that would change everything.

The third day of our counseling session was spent repenting and renouncing any areas the enemy had a hold in our lives. Renouncing breaks agreement with the enemy, thus taking back power he has stolen. By the end of the third day, I was feeling tired and thinking, "I wonder if anything is happening." I wanted to know, "Is this working?" We had been renouncing and declaring legal prayers, but I was not feeling different. Before I went to bed that night I prayed and asked God to show me what was happening in our sessions. I was exhausted and needed encouragement to keep going.

That night, I had a dream. In the dream, I was on my honeymoon with Pieter and we were swimming in the ocean. We were somewhere in the Caribbean. The water was crystal clear and we were swimming together. We could see each other perfectly under the water. We swam up to a small island, which was covered in white sand. The only thing on the small, tropical island was a house. The house had no windows or doors. There were white linen curtains hanging from the doors and windows and they were blowing and swaying in the warm, tropical breeze. The place looked like paradise. The only thing in the house was a bed. The bed was wood and it had four wooden posts with white linens hanging from them. White linens covered the bed. Perfectly placed at the center of the bed was a wooden box. Pieter and I went into the house and stood on opposite sides of the bed. I took the lid off the box and there was a huge black mamba snake in the box! I looked at Pieter and said, "We have to kill the snake." I reached my hand in the box and grabbed the snake, and Pieter grabbed the bottom of the snake. Suddenly, there was a knife in my hand and I used it to kill the snake. We put the snake back in the box and put the lid on the box and I woke up.

I immediately heard the Lord say to me, "Melinda, you are killing the snakes in your marriage! Keep going!" The snakes represented the enemy and his destruction he had done in our marriage. The white linens represented the purity that God was bringing back into our marriage bed. I looked up black mamba snakes on Google and learned that they are one of the deadliest snakes in the world. The Father was showing me what was happening in the spirit realm.

We were destroying the legal rights the enemy had to our lives! The Father spoke to me in such a personal way through that dream. I know now that He was teaching me about spiritual warfare.

"For we do not wrestle against flesh and blood, but against principalities, against powers, against the rulers of the darkness of this age, against spiritual hosts of wickedness in the heavenly places." Ephesians 6:12 NKJV

The battle Pieter and I were in was spiritual and it needed to be fought spiritually . Kris Vallotton from Bethel Church in Redding, California has said before, "We are in a battleship, not a cruise ship." And, I completely agree. Pieter and I were learning to look at our circumstances through spiritual eyes. We were in a spiritual battle and the battle was over our marriage.

The enemy does not play fair, and he often takes advantage of us when we are the most vulnerable - in our case during childhood. He had been lying to us our whole lives. He fed us so many lies, and we believed them because we were too young and vulnerable to fight back. The enemy is very opportunistic, but the more we become aware of his schemes, the stronger we become spiritually.

Our souls were actually oppressed because of the life we had lived prior to Jesus, and because of the things our family members had done. The soul is the filter to the heart. Therefore, whatever is left unhealed will flow into the heart.

The Demonically Oppressed Soul

Demonic oppression means demons are present inside of a person's body or soul. Yes, demons can and will dwell within the body and soul of a believer. For example, if a mother is pregnant with a child, but really does not want the baby, that child can actually experience feelings of rejection from the parent. The rejection they experience in the womb will follow them into adulthood. The foundation of that person's soul will be built on rejection instead of love. Demons of rejection can "hide out" in this person's life, making them feel rejected. Regardless of how many times they are told they are loved, they still feel rejected. This is because a door of opportunity was opened to the enemy in the womb. Rejection is a spirit and needs to be cast out. No amount of counseling or medication will ever make that person feel loved and accepted.

They need deliverance and healing in their soul.

Levels of oppression can vary from person to person, but rest assured that believers can never be possessed, because they are the possession of Christ. The enemy is ruthless, but demons cannot just do whatever they want. They need legal permission or "ground" to enter a person's life. Permission can look like unconfessed sin committed by the person or unconfessed sins in the generational line - sins that are passed down the person's bloodline.

The blood of Jesus covers our sins, but sins must be confessed for the blood of Jesus to have its full effect. "If we confess our sins, He is faithful and just to forgive us our sins and to cleanse us from all unrighteousness." I John 1:9 NKJV.

Sin creates openings for the enemy to oppress us, opening doors for demonic influence. The Apostle Paul warns the church in Ephesus not to give the devil a foothold or opportunity or accusation (see Ephesians 4:27). This implies that the enemy can have accusations against us if we allow it. The principle of "you reap what you sow" extends beyond the physical realm; it holds true in the spiritual realm (see Galatians 6:7).

Demons feed on garbage that is left unhealed. Demons are also referred to as rats in the Bible, and rats feed on garbage. Garbage can look like anger, bitterness, resentment, jealousy, trauma, and much more. When two people enter a marriage carrying deep emotional wounds, as Pieter and I did, they will struggle to truly connect. The problem is each person is focused on their own pain, which makes it difficult to see the other person clearly. Essentially, our hearts had a cloggy filter, so we were unable to connect the way God designed us to connect. We needed major soul healing before we could achieve the intimate connection we desired to have with each other.

Not everything is a demon, but many times the possibility of a spiritual source is overlooked. The church today is negatively impacted by a lack of awareness and action around demonic oppression. Many Christians do not understand or address the reality of spiritual warfare. As a result, demonic forces are able to influence and harm people in the church without being identified or resisted. Bringing these issues to light and equipping believers to combat oppression is key to strengthening the church. The condition of the church will improve as demonic oppression is acknowledged and addressed, rather than ignored. We know this personally, because we were oppressed.

The Power of Forgiveness

The fifth day of our inner healing and deliverance session was spent on forgiveness. We forgave everyone who had ever hurt us - the list was long! The question everyone asks me is - Melinda, how did you forgive Pieter? I learned, in our inner healing and deliverance session, that bitterness in the soul is like drinking poison and hoping you will get well. I was drinking a lot of poison. Unforgiveness and bitterness is legal ground for demons to oppress a person, and I was oppressed, bitter, and angry.

I was angry with Pieter and angry with the women he had been with. I had stuffed my pain so far down my soul that I was completely unaware of how angry I really was. It all came out in that office, and then I was faced with a choice. Would I hold on to my right to judge Pieter, or would I hand my right to judge over to Jesus? Would I continue to judge the women he had been with, or would I release them to Jesus?

Forgiveness takes power away from the enemy, and it frees us from a root of bitterness. Hebrews 12:15 says, "looking carefully lest anyone fall short of the grace of God; lest any root of bitterness springing up cause trouble, and by this many become defiled." Unforgiveness causes bitter roots to grow in our soul. Forgiveness means we lay the offense down at the feet of Jesus.

I released Pieter from his offense. I discovered the lies of unworthiness I had been believing and I had an encounter with the love of Jesus. I saw him holding me while I was a little girl. I realized He was always with me and had never left me. God's perfect love cast out all my fears of being vulnerable with Pieter.

The result of my choice to forgive was freedom for Pieter and freedom for myself. I also forgave and blessed the women he had slept with. Because of this choice I am no longer filled with bitterness, anger, or pain. I am completely free! "Therefore if the Son makes you free, you shall be free indeed." John 8:36 NKJV. Jesus is the only one who can truly heal our souls, but we have to choose to lay the pain down at His feet.

True forgiveness means we refuse to pick the offense back up and weaponize the past when it is convenient. Forgiving Pieter meant I was choosing not to pick up the offense again and remind Pieter of his mistakes when I was upset at him. I am thankful the Father never reminds me of all the things I have been forgiven of - the list would be long.

Loving Our Enemies

Loving our enemies is a sign that we truly love God with our whole heart. "You have heard that it was said, 'You shall love your neighbor and hate your enemy.' But I say to you, love your enemies, bless those who curse you, do good to those who hate you, and pray for those who spitefully use you and persecute you, that you may be sons of your Father in heaven; for He makes His sun rise on the evil and on the good, and sends rain on the just and on the unjust. For if you love those who love you, what reward have you? Do not even the tax collectors do the same?" Matthew 5:43-46 NKJV.

There are certain situations where we must walk away from individuals who have caused us pain. Certain relationships are toxic or dangerous, and should end. Forgiveness does not mean we do not have boundaries. Regardless of whether or not the relationship is restored, we are all called to forgive and bless those who curse us (see Luke 6:27-28).

Deliverance Day

The final day of our week-long inner healing and deliverance session was what I now call, "Deliverance Day." We had no idea what to expect, so I sat back in my chair, thankful that Pieter was going first. Jeanne began to call out different spirits such as lust, pornography, pride, anger, fear, etc. One by one, she commanded them to leave. Meanwhile, I felt a wave of nausea hit me like a brick wall. I thought, "Am I going to throw up?" I sat back in my chair and thought, "What is happening right now?! Why am I feeling so sick? Certainly, Jeanne must see that I am nauseous." I closed my eyes and contemplated running to the bathroom or grabbing the garbage can that sat in the corner. I sat and waited for Pieter's session to end - it felt like a lifetime of waiting!

Finally - Pieter's deliverance was complete. Pieter told me that he felt evil spirits leaving his body. It was my turn. Jeanne started calling out spirits and commanding them to leave. I could feel spirits leaving me. Each evil spirit left at her command. Rejection, fear, abandonment, anger, and so much more left me that day. I was crying as the weight I was carrying around began to leave. Deliverance is difficult to describe until you have been through it. You truly don't know what you are carrying until it's gone. I learned that the feelings of nausea I experienced were actually the demonic spirits in my body acting up because they were about to leave.

The next day we went to church and I felt peace I had never felt before. I cried softly as the worship music washed over me. I felt a tangible peace flowing through my body. I looked at Pieter and he was smiling back at me. He said, "It's gone! Whatever was making me want to look at pornography is gone!" We had no idea we had just won a major spiritual war. God had set us free! "Who the Son sets free is free indeed (see John 8:36)." And we were FREE!

The Unseen Realm

By recognizing the existence of the unseen realm around us — the realm of both heavenly and demonic influences — we can grasp the supreme reality of Jesus, His Kingdom, and His ability to set us free from every form of bondage. Jesus' primary ministry was healing people from physical conditions and casting out demons. The mandate has not changed, only now He partners with believers to see the captives free, and what an awesome privilege it is.

"…God anointed Jesus of Nazareth with the Holy Spirit and with power, and how he went about doing good and healing all who were under the tyranny of the devil, because God was with him." Acts 10:38 NKJV

Jesus came into the world with a divine purpose: to set us free both emotionally and physically (see Isaiah 61). God desires that we experience an abundant life filled with His blessing, provision, and goodness. "The thief does not come except to steal, and to kill, and to destroy. I have come that they may have life, and that they may have it more abundantly" (John 10:10 NKJV). The heart of the Father is to restore what the enemy has stolen. He is a jealous God and He wants all of us, healed, filled with joy, and made whole!

Jesus fulfilled His mission while He was here on earth, and He entrusted believers to do the same. He declared, "Most assuredly, I say to you, he who believes in Me, the works that I do he will do also; and greater works than these he will do, because I go to My Father" (John 14:12 NKJV). As believers, we are called to continue the ministry of Jesus, empowered by the Holy Spirit. We have been given authority over the works of darkness, including healing the sick, cleansing the leper, raising the dead, and casting out demons. (Matthew 10:8)

The transformative power we encountered during our six-day counseling session was nothing short of miraculous. Pieter was set free from the chains of sexual addiction and pornography, and I was liberated from a lifetime of anxiety, trauma, and emotional captivity. Our lives have been forever changed because of this profound experience. The Holy Spirit came in power to set us free and the restoration and freedom we have discovered is a testimony to the limitless power of the blood of Jesus.

"When the righteous cry for help, the Lord hears and delivers them out of all their troubles. The Lord is near to the brokenhearted and saves the crushed in spirit." Psalm 34:17-18 TPT

No matter your past experiences, know that you are not destined to bear the burden of oppression. Jesus came to set us free! We were never meant to live in captivity. Christ's sacrifice on the cross ensures that we can live a life overflowing with abundance. No matter the circumstances that have unfolded in your life, know that God is the ultimate restorer, redeemer, and rescuer. Jesus specializes in healing the brokenhearted, and Pieter and I once stood among them.

"The mighty Spirit of Lord Yahweh is wrapped around me, because Yahweh has anointed me, as a messenger to preach good news to the poor. He sent me to heal the wounds of the brokenhearted, to tell captives, 'You are free,' and to tell prisoners, 'Be free from your darkness.'" Isaiah 61:1 TPT

I pray that as you read this book you encounter the love of the Father. I pray that your heart is opened to the reality of what it means to live the abundant life (see John 10:10). I pray as you read this book your eyes will be opened to see the glorious inheritance that is available to you (Ephesians 1:18). I pray you receive revelation of the power of God that lives inside of you through His Holy Spirit, who dwells in all believers (1 Cor 3:16). I pray you know the plans God has for you will outweigh anything you could ask, think or imagine (Ephesians 3:20).

"Now to Him Who, by (in consequence of) the [action of His] power that is at work within us, is able to [carry out His purpose and] do superabundantly, far over and above all that we [dare] ask or think [infinitely beyond our highest prayers, desires, thoughts, hopes, or dreams]" Ephesians 3:20 AMPC

Chapter 3

The Believer's Authority

"Then the seventy returned with joy, saying, "Lord, even the demons are subject to us in Your name." And He said to them, "I saw Satan fall like lightning from heaven. Behold, I give you the authority to trample on serpents and scorpions, and over all the power of the enemy, and nothing shall by any means hurt you. Nevertheless do not rejoice in this, that the spirits are subject to you, but rather rejoice because your names are written in heaven."

Luke 10:17-20 NKJV

Pieter and I were so radically transformed after our deliverance that our hearts burned to bring the same freedom to others. We began to consume books, sermons, and podcasts on deliverance. Our hunger to see the captives set free could not be quenched. We shared our testimony of freedom whenever we had an opportunity. People started coming to us to ask for prayers for freedom. When people came to us and asked for deliverance, we said yes. Our hearts yearned to see others experience the gift of freedom we had experienced.

Just a few months after we were set free, we had a married couple sitting in our home office. They were desperate for freedom, just like we were. They attended ministry school with us and sought us out after hearing our testimony of God delivering us. We were nervous about leading the couple through inner healing and deliverance because it was our first time ministering to a married couple. We prepared ourselves with prayer and fasting. We were praying that God would meet them powerfully.

So many lies surfaced during the session for me, "Am I qualified to do this? Will God show up in power like he did in our session? Will God use little old me to set the captives free?"

We spent two days leading the couple into freedom through inner healing and deliverance under the guidance of the Holy Spirit. We learned the couple did not grow up in the church. They were first-generation believers. The husband was addicted to pornography. He was also struggling with lust and had been sexually abused as a child. The wife had practiced witchcraft as a psychic for years before she married her husband and before they were saved and came to ministry school together.

We began to pray as we led the couple through deliverance. The demons tried to cause a scene. The wife took on the form of a snake and hissed at us as we ministered freedom to her. Usually, there are minimal manifestations. Although there was no physical evidence, the husband told us after the deliverance that he could feel the evil spirits leaving his body as we prayed. By the end of the session, the couple was free from torment, and filled with the Holy Spirit. The wife was filled with laughter and tears as she testified about her encounter. She saw Jesus standing before her, reaching out His hand, and could feel the release she had experienced because of His goodness.

Pieter and I cried, watching the power of Jesus set this amazing couple free. We were in awe of God's love. Thinking that Jesus would use us to help bring freedom to other people is a privilege and honor that we will never take for granted.

Learning about Spiritual Authority

From that moment on, God started speaking to me about my authority. We had multiple deliverance sessions where I was questioning my authority to cast out demons. Each time I ministered deliverance, another person was always in the room, mainly Pieter. I always believed that Pieter was more anointed than me and that demons were leaving because of Pieter's authority. I had a stronghold of doubt that needed to be torn down! But God orchestrated a divine setup!

I had the opportunity to travel during my time in ministry school. On one occasion, I traveled to another state to speak with a few other women at a women's conference. The women leading the event discovered that Pieter and I had an inner healing and deliverance ministry. The leaders had been trained in this area but were hungry to grow and learn more. They asked if they could set up a special teaching session for me to teach on deliverance. I had two hours' notice to prepare! I was nervous, but I said yes.

I walked into the room to teach on deliverance, and there were about thirty women waiting who came for the bonus teaching. I heard the Lord say to me, "Teach what you know. You know how to do this!" I said yes to the Lord in my heart. I had no idea that God was setting me up.

I did a short teaching on deliverance and answered a few questions from some of the women. Then someone asked the question that changed everything, "Can you pray for us to receive deliverance?" I was nervous about the question. I looked at the leaders, and they agreed and said it was a good idea. I said silently to the Lord, "What do I do? I have never prayed deliverance for a group!?" The Lord said, "Start by renouncing any witchcraft in the family line. Just like we do it when we pray for people at home." I responded silently, "Yes, Lord! That's a great idea!"

I explained to the women that I would lead them through a prayer and told them they might not feel anything but to trust that the Lord would set them free if they needed freedom in that area. I was nervous but moved forward with faith as I prayed. I had the women repeat a prayer, renouncing any witchcraft, and then I commanded all demonic spirits to come forward and come out. For a few minutes, nothing happened. I prayed, "Help, Holy Spirit!" the whole time. Sometimes, "Help, Holy Spirit!" is the most effective prayer. We can't do anything without His presence.

Suddenly, a woman in the corner started manifesting and her face contorted demonically. I had a friend present with me, and she walked over to the woman and asked me to come over and assist her. The woman slithered to the ground from her chair in the form of a snake. We spent about twenty minutes casting demons out of the woman, and she was completely set free! Later in the week, several other women received deliverance. We did not even pray for them to be delivered. They just started manifesting during worship! Demons were fleeing in the thick presence of God!

God spoke to me so clearly about my authority through these events. "Melinda, you are anointed for this purpose! Trust that I am with you!" The Lord spoke directly into my heart; I have never been the same again since this experience. Any doubt I had was destroyed as I saw those women set free that weekend.

Since this time, I have ministered freedom to hundreds of individuals. People keep coming to me. Regardless of how anointed I feel, I keep saying yes. I say yes to whoever the Lord leads me to pray for. I have learned that to have breakthrough in areas where we feel unqualified requires stepping out and "doing it afraid." Stepping out requires trusting the Holy Spirit, even when we do not feel anointed or powerful.

The anointing on a believer is the Holy Spirit, and the Holy Spirit is a person. Having a relationship with the Holy Spirit is crucial for life and ministry. I could not do a single deliverance without the Holy Spirit's presence and power. The Holy Spirit must be our compass as we minister in love, as nothing worthy can be done in our own strength without His presence.

Doing what Jesus Did - The Great Commission

As believers, we are all commissioned to do what Jesus did. Jesus' idea of moving in love and compassion was to move in power and authority by setting the captives free. Jesus never once sent His disciples out to minister without the power of the Holy Spirit. Jesus said, "Behold, I give you the authority to trample on serpents and scorpions, and over all the power of the enemy, and nothing shall by any means hurt you." Luke 10:19 NKJV. As believers in Jesus Christ, we do not need to be afraid of the Devil, because he was defeated at the cross. "[God] disarmed the principalities and powers that were ranged against us and made a bold display and public example of them, in triumphing over them in Him and in it [the cross]." Colossians 2:15 AMPC.

I have heard people say that we need to focus on Jesus and ignore the Devil. Of course, we should keep our gaze focused on Jesus, but let's remember the life of Jesus. What did Jesus do exactly?

"How God anointed Jesus of Nazareth with the Holy Spirit and with power, who went about doing good and healing all who were oppressed by the devil, for God was with Him." Acts 10:38 NKJV

Jesus walked around destroying the works of the devil, which included casting out demons, healing the sick, cleansing the leper, and raising the dead. Jesus only did what He saw the Father doing, which meant He was focused on the Father's will while He was here on earth. Jesus would pray and spend time with the Father, then go back out and do what He was commissioned to do, which was to bring heaven to earth (see Matthew 6:10).

Jesus demonstrated true love by healing the oppressed and casting out demons.

Freedom is the Father's will for His children. Jesus was a disrupter of hell's agenda, and so are we. After His resurrection, Jesus said to His disciples in the great commission in Matthew 28:18-20: "And Jesus came and spoke to them, saying, "Jesus came and told his disciples, "I have been given all authority in heaven and on earth. Therefore, go and make disciples of all the nations, baptizing them in the name of the Father and the Son and the Holy Spirit. Teach these new disciples to obey all the commands I have given you. And be sure of this: I am with you always, even to the end of the age." Matthew 28:18-20 NLT

Jesus specifically commanded his disciples to do what He had taught them, including in large part, healing the sick and casting out demons. We see the disciples (his church) commissioned again in Matthew 10:8:

"And as you go, preach, saying, 'The kingdom of heaven is at hand.' Heal the sick, cleanse the lepers, raise the dead, cast out demons. Freely you have received, freely give." Matthew 10:7-8 NKJV

Jesus only sent His disciples out to do ministry with the power of the Holy Spirit! Think about that truth. The disciples were always filled with the power of the Holy Spirit, which gave them the ability to cast out demons, heal the sick, raise the dead, and cleanse the leper. The commission has stayed the same today. When we are set free, we can set others free, too! What a joy it is to see chains of oppression ripped from the body of Christ.

My heart burns to see others set free because there is nothing like freedom. I was once captive, but JESUS set me free. Pieter and I needed emotional healing and deliverance. We did not need another sermon or counseling appointment. Of course, counseling has its place as well as sermons, but those things would not remove a yoke of demonic oppression.

The Power of the Holy Spirit

When the Lord poured out His Spirit at Pentecost (see Acts 1-2), we were given access to the Holy Spirit and His power to destroy the works of the enemy by setting people free. "You shall receive power (ability, efficiency, and might) when the Holy Spirit has come upon you, and you shall be my witnesses in Jerusalem and Judea and Samaria and the ends (the very bounds) of the earth. (AMPC, Acts 1:8). The word "power" in Greek is the word dunamis, which means; force, miraculous power, miracle, power, strength, violence, and wonder, moral power and excellence of soul."

Sanctification

When Pieter and I gave our lives to Jesus, we thought everything would feel new and perfect. The Bible says we are a new creation (2 Corinthians 5:17), so we expected to feel like a new creation. However, no one told us that although we are a new creation, there would be a sanctification process where we would work out our salvation, which might include the need for inner healing and deliverance.

When we are born again, the Holy Spirit comes to dwell inside of us. We become the righteousness of Christ. However, our souls, our mind, will, and emotions still need to be sanctified. The blood of Jesus covers our sins, but for the blood to have its full effect, we must renounce any legal partnerships made by us or by the generations before us. "When we renounce our sins, he is faithful and just to forgive us our sins and to cleanse us from all unrighteousness (1 John 1:9)." Sanctification is "the action or process of being freed from sin or purified" (Oxford Dictionary). Sanctification begins at salvation. Justification happens the moment we are saved. When we are immediately justified when we are born again, but we are being sanctified or "purified."

"Now may the God of peace himself sanctify you completely, and may your whole spirit and soul be kept blameless at the coming of our Lord Jesus Christ." 1 Thessalonians 5:23 NKJV

This scripture was written to a church full of born-again believers. When we are born again, we are saved. We will go to heaven when we die, but the blood of Jesus and the dunamis power of the resurrection is what will set us free. With the awareness of the sanctification process, which sometimes includes deliverance, our journey with Jesus will be more joy-filled and more satisfying.

"My people are destroyed for lack of knowledge." Hosea 4:6 NKJV

After Pieter and I were born again, we lacked this awareness, which caused us to feel tired, burned out, and frustrated. We had no idea we needed sanctification through deliverance and healing in our souls. The problem today is that most believers have yet to fully realize the work of the blood of Jesus and the power of the resurrection in every area of their heart, soul, and mind - our inner man. Without teaching believers their need for sanctification, we will continue to see "unbelieving believers" who are burned out, frustrated, and weary. We desperately need the blood of Jesus and the dunamis power of the Holy Spirit to set us free.

Christians can be demonically oppressed or demonized. When Pieter and I came to ministry school, we had no idea that we needed to be delivered. We learned that the work of sanctification is a journey that begins at the moment of salvation and is not instantaneous. Dr. Randy Clark says, "Deliverance is part of the sanctification process." (The Biblical Guidebook for Deliverance). Deliverance removes demonic strongholds hidden in areas of our soul (our mind, will, and emotions) and sometimes in our physical bodies.

The blood of Jesus cleanses us from all unrighteousness, and the power of the Holy Spirit, the anointing sets us free. Isaiah 10:27 says, "The anointing breaks the yoke." Believers need the blood of Jesus and the resurrection power of the Holy Spirit to set them free. Acts 10:38 says, "How God anointed Jesus of Nazareth with the Holy Spirit and with power, who went about doing good and healing all who were oppressed by the devil, for God was with Him." The word "power" is the Greek word "dunamis" (doo'-nam-is) (Strong's G1411).

"He who sins is of the devil, for the devil has sinned from the beginning. For this purpose, the Son of God was manifested, that He might destroy the works of the devil." I John 3:8 NKJV

Loving the Body of Christ through Deliverance

Simply put, deliverance aims to uncover what is oppressing an individual by revealing what particular spirit has a right to be there. The ultimate goal is to cast the spirit out or expel the demon. The mission of deliverance is to uncover the strongholds in the person's life. Deliverance should always be done in LOVE. Speaking with authority can be necessary, but yelling is never necessary. Demons do not respond to yelling; they respond to the authority of the anointed believer, and demons know and recognize the difference. The anointing breaks the yoke of oppression (see Isaiah 10:27). The anointing is the Holy Spirit's presence resting on the believer's life.

On one occasion, we ministered to a woman attending her first year of ministry school. She had been baptized in water and the Holy Spirit, but she still struggled with unreasonable fear and had nightmares, among many other issues. We brought her in for a deliverance session and discovered that she had a family history of occult practices and struggled with abandonment, rejection, and fear. She was also abused as a child and molested. Any time there is sexual abuse, occult, or sexual sin, you will find demonic company.

We ministered to the woman for two hours and uncovered the demons afflicting and tormenting her soul. We discovered that the woman had unforgiveness towards her father, who had abused her physically, and unforgiveness towards the person who had abused her sexually. She was also believing many lies about who God was as her protector.

Victims of these awful crimes often hold onto bitterness, believing that holding on to the pain is their right. However, the truth is unforgiveness causes a bitter root to grow in our soul, preventing us from progressing in Christ. Forgiveness means we give up our right to hold the other person accountable. We release the person to Jesus and ask Him to take the pain of the offense away. Forgiveness is the highest form of mercy, and it is an active choice to lay the offense at the feet of Jesus. Forgiveness releases the other person, and frees us from a root of bitterness. (See Chapter 7 on The Power of Forgiveness).

"Pursue peace with all people, and holiness, without which no one will see the Lord: looking carefully lest anyone fall short of the grace of God; lest any root of bitterness springing up cause trouble, and by this many become defiled;" Hebrews 12:14-15 NKJV

"For if you forgive men their trespasses, your heavenly Father will also forgive you. But if you do not forgive men their trespasses, neither will your Father forgive your trespasses." Matthew 6:14-15 NKJV

Can a Demon Possess a Christian?

Demons cannot possess Christians because that would mean a Christian was the possession of the Devil. The Bible is clear that we are Christ's possession from the moment we are born again. However, Christians can be "oppressed" by demons or "demonized." When we are born again by the Spirit of God (see John 3), we become heirs to the Kingdom. In one radical moment, we are transferred from the kingdom of darkness into the Kingdom of the Son of His love (see Colossians 1:13). We are saved from the moment we believe and confess with our mouths and believe in our hearts that Jesus died and rose from the dead. This is what it means to be "born again." You are spiritually born into the Kingdom of God (see John 3:3). You become a new creation! Romans 10:13 says, "Everyone who calls upon the name of the Lord will be saved." Salvation is a gift from God, not from our works or striving.

"For it was only through this wonderful grace that we believed in Him. Nothing we did could ever earn this salvation, for it was the gracious gift from God that brought us to Christ!" Ephesians 2:8 TPT

John 19:30, Jesus says, "It is finished." Our salvation was "paid in full." This phrase appeared on the back of first-century legal documents, indicating that a debt had been paid in full. The blood of Jesus paid for our salvation. However, as Paul said to the church at Philippi, we must work out our salvation with fear and trembling (Philippians 2:12). Does this mean we have to work on being saved? Of course not! Salvation is a gift given by God's grace (His divine empowerment), but sin does have spiritual consequences that may not always disappear at the moment of salvation.

Although we are saved from the moment we are born again, we are continuously in a sanctification process. Deliverance from demonic oppression is part of the sanctification process. Lack of this awareness is why Pieter and I felt so terrible, even after being saved! We needed to be emotionally healed and delivered from demonic oppression.

"Now, may the God of peace himself sanctify you completely. And may your whole spirit, soul, and body be kept sound and blameless at the coming of our Lord Jesus Christ." 1 Thessalonians 5:23 NKJV

Possession or Oppression?

Dr. Randy Clark explains the difference between being oppressed by a demon and possessed. "I do not believe a Christian can be totally demonized, and I do not believe that a Christian can be possessed. The Bible says that we have been bought with a price, the precious blood of Jesus Christ. We are His possessions. Therefore, we can never become the enemy's possession, nor can we be totally possessed by the enemy if we are born again. That being said, I do not believe a Christian can be possessed according to what is usually understood by the term possessed. However, I do believe a Christian can be demonized or influenced by evil spirits. Wilber said it this way: he did not believe a demon could have or "own" a Christian because he didn't believe a demon could possess a Christian. If we are born again, we belong to Christ. Therefore a demon cannot own us or possess us. So, even though a demon cannot have a Christian, a Christian can have a demon." We need to develop the spiritual habit of a biblical response to the trials of life so that the enemy cannot find any open door through which he can bring oppression to our souls. (The Biblical Guidebook to Deliverance, Randy Clark DMin.).

The process of removing demonic oppression involves closing open "doors" that were opened to the enemy. "Doors" are a metaphor for an opening or access point. The goal in deliverance is to close the demonic doors we opened through believing a lie, sinning, participating in the occult, generational sins (iniquities), fear, or bitterness and unforgiveness. Unless we repent for and renounce our sins, the enemy still has a legal right to "camp" like an illegal squatter in those areas of our soul. The good news is the Lord promises: "If we confess our sins, He is faithful and just to forgive us our sins and cleanse us from all unrighteousness." (1 John 1:9). The key here is IF we confess our sins. Sins must be confessed (renounced) for Jesus' blood to cleanse us from all unrighteousness.

Jesus also teaches us that we can be bound by what we believe or do not believe. "Then Jesus said to those Jews who believed Him, "If you abide in My word, you are My disciples indeed. And you shall know the truth, and the truth shall make you free." John 8:31-32 NKJV. Strongholds are formed when we believe lies, and those lies become truth to us. One of the keys in deliverance is to uncover the lies the individual is believing and replace the lies with the truth. Jesus came to destroy the works of the devil (1 John 3:8). The remedy is to cast out the demons in Jesus' name, and Jesus gave believers the authority to cast out demons. "But if I cast out demons with the finger of God, surely the Kingdom of God has come upon you." Luke 11:20. "No demon can remain when a Christian seriously desires him to go! 'Resist the devil and he will flee from you.' (James 4:7b)." Frank Hammond, Pigs in the Parlor.

The enemy is always looking for an opportunity to take up territory in our souls. "Watch out for the enemy who walks around like a roaring lion looking for someone to devour." (see 1 Peter 5:8). We see the enemy tempting the hearts of believers in the account of Ananias and Sapphira. "Ananias," Peter asked, "Why has Satan filled your heart to lie to the Holy Spirit and keep back part of the proceeds of the land?" Acts 5:3 CSB. Ananias partnered with Satan in a plan to lie and hide proceeds from a land sale from the Apostles. Satan looked for someone to devour and found that Ananias was willing to partner with him and fall into sin. The temptation was to lie over money, costing him his life and the life of his wife, Sapphira.

"Why did you agree to test the Spirit of the Lord? Look, the feed of those who have buried your husband are at the doors, and they will carry you out. Instantly, she dropped dead at his feet..." Acts 5:9 TPT

This example is extreme, but it is a spiritual truth and was included in the New Testament for a reason. I believe the story of Ananias and Sapphira demonstrates what happens when we have an unrepentant heart. We essentially die inside and cut ourselves off from receiving God's grace and mercy. Not because His grace and mercy aren't available but because we refuse to lay down our pride, humble ourselves, turn to the Lord and repent. Romans 2:4 says it is the goodness of God that leads to repentance. The word "repent" means to turn away from something, and to change the way we think. When God invites us to repent He is inviting us to turn from our old way of thinking. He is inviting us to see the truth from His perspective.

Captives in the Church

Deliverance and inner healing are for the church and are greatly needed. People in church are suffering and are in desperate need of freedom. Deliverance is not reserved for special people with deliverance ministries. Pieter and I are passionate about teaching others what we have learned so they can go out and set the captives free. We consider our ministry, "Arise and Shine Ministries," a teaching and "equipping the saints" ministry. Jesus came into a demon-possessed world as the Son of God and spent three years teaching us a model for deliverance. He even said we would do greater things (see John 14:12). Jesus is the perfect model for life as a believer. He healed many physically set many people free from demonic torment, and we are commissioned to do the same!

"He who believes and is baptized will be saved; but he who does not believe will be condemned. And these signs will accompany those who believe: In my name they will drive out demons; they will speak in new tongues; they will pick up snakes with their hands; and when the drink deadly poison, it will not hurt them at all; they will place their hands on sick people, and they will get well." Mark 16:17 NIV

What are Demons?

Demons are spirits without bodies, which is why they look to inhabit bodies of humans (Ephesians 6:12 and Mathew 12:43-45). They are intelligent and know your history. They have a will and resist surrender.

Demons fear God and His Word, they fear believers who know their authority. Demons are highly organized and look to do as much destruction as possible to advance the kingdom of Satan. They also know their time is short. Demons have emotions and tremble in fear around anointed believers (James 2:19). They are restless and they can speak. They have one goal in mind - to steal, kill and destroy humans (John 10:10).

Demons are legalistic and can only occupy humans when allowed through sin or agreement. Demons are not all-powerful and they have to bow to the blood of Jesus. They know this, but they will try to intimidate believers in a deliverance session. We have seen this many times before when a person starts speaking in demonic tongues or starts barking at us.

How Do You Know If You Need Deliverance?

- Isolation (from family or others)
- Addictions - loss of personal control
- Appetites out of control - sexual, fleshly
- Behavior extremes - something comes over the person
- Deceitful personality
- Humiliation
- A drive or obsessive thoughts to do something terrible
- Occultic Involvement (generational involvement or self)
- Violent Tendencies (self-harming)
- Hearing Voices
- Mental illness (although it is important to note that not all mental illness is demonic in origin)

My personal experience of being set free from demonic oppression and the example of Jesus' ministry in the Bible demonstrates that you can be set free from anxiety, fear, rejection, abandonment, depression, lust, pornography addiction, shame, and so much more! Pieter and I feel like entirely different people today, and we now understand what Jesus meant when He said He came to set the captives free (see Luke 6 and Isaiah 61).

"The Spirit of the Lord God is on me because the Lord has anointed me to bring good news to the poor (poor in spirit). He has sent me to heal the broken-hearted (emotionally hurting), to proclaim liberty to the captives (emotional freedom), and freedom to the prisoners; to proclaim in the year of the Lord's favor, and the day of our God's vengeance; to comfort all who mourn, to provide for those who mourn in Zion; to give a crown of beauty instead of ashes, festive oil (the Holy Spirit) instead of mourning, and splendid clothes instead of despair. And they (believers) will be called righteous trees, planted by the Lord to glorify Him." Isaiah 61:1-3 (emphasis mine)

Jesus paid the ultimate price so that we could walk in freedom. Jesus came to set us free from emotional, spiritual, and physical bondage, and He taught us how to lead others into freedom. Jesus came: "To destroy the works of the devil" (See 1 John 3:8)! Jesus setting us free is entirely by grace. We can do nothing to earn grace, or be "good enough." All that is required for freedom is a humble, willing heart. We cannot earn our way into being saved or delivered, otherwise, the work of the cross would mean nothing.

You might be asking yourself if you have gone too far or done too much for the grace of God to forgive you, heal you, and restore you. Let's cover that subject as we read about Jesus, and the woman caught in adultery.

"At dawn he appeared again in the temple courts, where all the people gathered around him, and he sat down to teach them. The teachers of the law and the Pharisees brought in a woman caught in adultery. They made her stand before the group and said to Jesus, "Teacher, this woman was caught in the act of adultery. In the Law Moses commanded us to stone such women. Now what do you say?" They were using this question as a trap, in order to have a basis for accusing him. But Jesus bent down and started to write on the ground with his finger. When they kept on questioning him, he straightened up and said to them, "Let any one of you who is without sin be the first to throw a stone at her." Again he stooped down and wrote on the ground. At this, those who heard began to go away one at a time, the older ones first, until only Jesus was left, with the woman still standing there. Jesus straightened up and asked her, "Woman, where are they? Has no one condemned you?" "No one, sir," she said. "Then neither do I condemn you," Jesus declared. "Go now and leave your life of sin." John 8:2-11 NIV

The religious leaders caught the woman "in the act of adultery." Although the Bible doesn't specify, I sometimes wonder if she had clothes on or if they dragged her naked in front of the crowd. She was likely so ashamed of what she had done. She was then brought to the temple to potentially face her death by stoning. The woman was likely full of fear. But Jesus saw her, and He covered her by forgiving her sins. He also called out the hypocrisy of the religious leaders who had also sinned. I believe Jesus' words were so powerful when he spoke to the woman that He delivered her from her desire to sin.

If Jesus can forgive a woman caught in adultery and forgive "Saul" who turned into the Apostle Paul, who was ruthlessly murdering Christians, He is willing to forgive us too! And not only forgive us but restore us to better than before - as though it never happened! There is no striving to earn this gift of grace that comes from our heavenly Father. Jesus can and will set you free.

"Come to me, all of you who are weary and burdened, and I will give you rest. Take my yoke and l earn from me, because I am lowly and humble in heart and you will find rest for your souls." Matthew 11:28-29 NIV

Chapter 4

Healing the Wounded Soul

"The Lord is my shepherd; I shall not want. He makes me to lie down in green pastures; He leads me beside the still waters. He restores my soul; He leads me in the paths of righteousness For His name's sake. Yea, though I walk through the valley of the shadow of death, I will fear no evil; For You are with me; Your rod and Your staff, they comfort me. You prepare a table before me in the presence of my enemies; You anoint my head with oil; My cup runs over. Surely goodness and mercy shall follow me All the days of my life; And I will dwell in the house of the Lord Forever."

Psalms 23:1-6 NKJV

When Pieter and I married, we still carried a tremendous amount of emotional baggage from our past. We both longed to not carry this baggage and somewhere deep in us we were hoping that when we married each other this baggage would somehow go away. In spite of our best intentions to marry and give ourselves wholly to each other in honor, the pain from this emotional baggage manifested in very negative ways, leaving both of us frustrated and exhausted. We loved each other deeply, but we were processing that love through our unhealed pain. We tried many different methods to heal our marriage, but didn't yet understand that real change required deep healing within our souls.

After Pieter was radically saved, and before inner healing and deliverance, Pieter pursued counseling, men's groups, and seminars - yet nothing brought lasting freedom. The stronghold of porn and lust was only being suppressed.

Pieter would repeatedly go to altar calls for freedom and even rededication to Jesus. Pieter was desperate and he has said before lost in a state of "I can't fix this so what am I to do?"

We have learned that you can't counsel a demon. It was like Pieter had this metaphorical "broken leg" preventing him from running freely. In order to not exacerbate this broken leg, Pieter used all sorts of "crutches" to not feel the pain or make the broken leg worse. Pieter's broken leg is the metaphor of his soul before he was saved, healed, and delivered. The metaphor of his crutches were all the things he was doing in his own strength without a deeper surrender to allow Jesus to deliver him from this stronghold and into freedom.

Even after we both experienced this freedom we still faced people who would ask, "How do you know you are really free?" Pieter once redirected this question to God because honestly he didn't know how he knew, he just knew. God spoke to Pieter about the word freedom. Freedom is two words. Free and dominion. God explained that by giving His heart and mind to Jesus Pieter was in the Kingdom. Kingdom is also two words. King and dominion and Kingdom is a place, while freedom is a state. Both Kingdom and freedom go hand in hand. You can't have one without the other. Pieter had a tremendous revelation that being in the dominion of the King meant that he was free from dominion of the demonic. After inner healing and deliverance we both developed an authority and revelation that our no to the demonic was just as powerful as our yes to Jesus.

What is Inner Healing?

Inner healing is the deepest form of soul healing - healing the mind, will, and emotions. Inner healing and deliverance should be ministered together. Otherwise, you might heal a wound without casting out a spirit that is present, or you might cast something out without healing the wound. The goal of inner healing is to look at the individual's story and heal any wounds that might be present in the soul. Inner healing heals the deepest part of our soul - our inner man. Simply put, inner healing heals the wounds in the soul, and deliverance casts out spirits from the person's body and soul.

Healing the Soul - Intimacy is Key

Healing the wounds in our soul is important, but all of our pain should be processed with the Lord. We are His beloved children. He wants conversation with us and a deep heart connection more than He wants to "repair us." We are not broken machines, but children of God. As you read this chapter, bring all of your issues to the Lord. He cares for you. Jesus said, "Take My yoke upon you and learn from Me, for I am gentle and lowly in heart, and you will find rest for your souls." Matthew 11:29 NKJV. Process your story with the Lord. It is His will to bring you in close and care for you like a loving Father.

I still had pain that I needed to process after I went through inner healing and deliverance. The first time we were with an inner healing and deliverance counselor, and that was an amazing experience. We couldn't have done it without her help. But after the initial help, the Father wanted me to come to Him to deal with other issues of my heart. I would sit with the Father early in the morning and let His love wash over me. He would speak to my heart and I would leave feeling loved, affirmed, and chosen.

The Father takes great joy in spending time with us. If the idea of going to the Father is new to you simply start with a journal and bible. Talk to Him and share your heart. Prayer is not a formula, rather a relationship. Keep it simple and try to get into a quiet space and relax.

The story you are about to read can bring up soul issues that need to be healed. Write down anything that comes up that needs healing. Consider bringing a friend into the journey to share what you are processing, but don't allow your time with a friend to compromise your time with the Lord. Also, remember that healing takes time, so allow yourself time to process pain and for the Father to heal the pain of the past.

Celebrate and know that you can be filled with joy again. The Lord can and will heal your heart and soul. Trust Jesus as you lean into the process of inner healing. He restores our soul (Psalm 23). That is a promise from the Father! So take heart as you read through this chapter. The Father is with you as you read these pages.

Wounded William

The enemy uses several tactics to destroy our lives, relationships, and loved ones, but we are going to focus on the story of "Wounded William," which demonstrates how the demonic can occupy and oppress our souls. "Wounded William" is not a real person but is made up of several of the individuals we have ministered inner healing and deliverance to over the years.

William grew up in a relatively "normal" home, but William's life turned upside down when his parents began to fight and eventually divorced when he was eight years old. William was bullied at school around the same time. He went to his father for advice, and his father laughed at him and told him he needed to get tough and fight back. Wounded William was called "stupid, dumb, loser," among many things, throughout his childhood. William did not have many friends in school, and he often felt very alone.

William's parents remained divorced, and his mom eventually remarried and moved away to another state. As a result, Wounded William was often left home alone while his Dad worked long hours that often went into the night. William's Dad would take him to church on Sundays and his family called themselves Christians, but there was no real demonstration of love, faith, or fatherly love at home. Eventually, William's uncle would stop by when his Dad was gone and started sexually abusing him. William was too embarrassed to tell his Dad, so he kept the abuse a secret. William eventually started attending a youth group with a friend, and decided he wanted to become a pastor because he loved being in church and feeling loved, safe, and seen. William would go to youth groups on and off for the next several years.

But despite the church community, William was still lonely and didn't feel seen. He eventually got his first cell phone and discovered pornography during high school. William started watching porn regularly to cope with his feelings of loneliness to numb the pain in his heart. He eventually went to Bible college and got involved in sexual relationships with different women to feel wanted, accepted, and desired because deep in his heart Wounded William was afraid of being alone, abandoned and rejected.

Shame and guilt would always set in a few hours after he looked at porn or slept with someone. Thoughts came in from the enemy such as, "I am a Christian, why cant I stop watching porn and having sex? I am such a hypocrite! I am a terrible pastor! What I have done is too big to receive forgiveness for and it will never be redeemed." The accusations seemed to scream in his ear. The very demons that coerced William or "hooked" him into watching porn and having sex were now using guilt, fear, and shame to keep Wounded William feeling bad about himself. Those same lying demons used shame to keep Wounded William in a state of hopeless hiding. William began to get angry, just like his Dad.

What was Wounded William to do? He was afraid to talk to anyone about his lifestyle and the abuse he experienced as a child. He felt hopeless, undeserving and out of control. Wounded William was stuck in a cycle of sin, and he felt like he could not escape. He would hear thoughts like, "I am just like my Dad! I hate myself!"

Demonic Oppression

The problem is Wounded William had come under a demonic stronghold. The urge to look at pornography and to lust after women felt all too real. By sinning, he signed the demonic contract of pornography, lust, sex, abuse, and fear, among many other things. Our actions can signify a legal agreement with people and with the demonic. Wounded William's sinful actions gave the enemy the legal right to harass him from the inside of his soul. Demons also entered through the sexual abuse Wounded William experienced - this is demonic oppression. This is how the enemy can hook us, as it is very hard to "resist the devil" when the enemy is harassing us from the inside our souls. The enemy took advantage of Wounded William when he was the most vulnerable - during his childhood.

There is always a source to why we do what we do. The root of William's sinful lifestyle went back to childhood. Wounded William had no one to talk to or to share his heart with. He felt abandoned and alone when his parents divorced, when his mom moved away, and when he was bullied by boys at school. When Wounded William was sexually abused he felt deep guilt and shame from those traumatic events and made a vow, "I will never tell anyone about this". Wounded William had repented each time he sinned as an adult, so why did he still feel so bad? The problem was, although he had repented for the sin, the demonic stronghold in his soul was rooted in the lie and vow that William believed as a boy. This belief continued into adulthood. "I am alone and not worthy of being accepted or sought after. So, I will never lose control and take care of myself. I can't trust God because He did not protect me or prevent this from happening." Without renouncing the vow and the abuse, the demonic stronghold remained in his soul, keeping him bound to the lie.

Over time Wounded William allowed bitterness and unforgiveness into his heart and soul. He struggled to forgive the boys who were mean to him, his parents for abandoning him and for getting a divorce, and God. Wounded William slowly positioned his heart away from God to protect his heart from pain. Over the years, the joy and thankfulness William once had, were replaced with bitterness and unforgiveness.

Knowing Your Story

My story was similar to Wounded William's. I was deeply hurt when I was a young girl. Thankfully, I was not sexually abused, and my parents loved me. But they divorced when I was nine years old. I was the oldest child and I believed that it was my responsibility to take care of everyone - my parents included. Because of the circumstances, I believed the lie that I had to perform for love. Because the wound in my soul was not healed, I eventually moved into a sinful lifestyle because my heart was looking to fill a void for love. During my session with Pieter, I discovered the lies I had been believing and the truth that God really loved me and wanted to heal the wounds in my heart and soul and comfort me in my place of pain.

"He heals the broken-hearted and binds up their wounds." Psalm 147:3 NKJV

The Power of Agreement

The spirit realm feeds on agreement. Like Wounded William, I felt rejected, unworthy, and alone, so I made a vow without even realizing I had made it: "I am alone, so I will always have to take care of myself and perform for love." I had an encounter with Jesus when I went through inner healing and deliverance in that little office in Redding, California, that changed my life forever. I could finally see that Jesus was there through it all. I saw the Truth that He never left me! I saw Jesus with me as a child. He held me in His arms. I had the personal revelation that He was always there. I replaced the lie that I was alone with the Truth of God's promise: "I will never leave you or forsake you." (See Deuteronomy 31:6).

I also renounced the vow that I had made: "I am alone, so I will always have to take care of myself and perform for love." Once I identified the lie and vow I had partnered with as a young girl, we replaced it with the truth, taking power away from the enemy. Then, the enemy was cast out of my soul. "If you confess your sins he is faithful and just to cleanse you from all unrighteousness." (1 John 1:9). The truth was, God is with me and He will never leave me.

Sin is a Heart Issue

Our hearts long to be loved, accepted, wanted, and cherished. When the desires of our hearts are not met through Jesus, we will look for fulfillment in other areas. Sin is birthed from an unfulfilled heart need. I slept with men at a young age outside of marriage because I wanted to fulfill my heart's desire to be loved, approved, accepted, and cherished. When those needs went unmet, I would look for fulfillment in the wrong places. Sin is always an issue of the heart. Even the worst sins you could imagine were usually birthed from someone not being loved, cherished, or cared for as a child.

The Love of Jesus

Because sin is an issue of the heart, deliverance, and inner healing must always be done in love. We are all longing to be loved and accepted. Deliverance is about removing the destruction of the enemy and replacing it with the love of Jesus. For this reason, when done together, inner healing and deliverance are powerful. What is cast out must be filled with the truth of God's word and the love of Christ. Deliverance casts out what evil is present, and fills the heart with love. Deep down, we are all longing to be loved and accepted.

The Courts of Heaven

The demonic realm and the heavenly realm are like a court system. When you commit a sin, you need an advocate and a defender for your court case (Jesus) to come in and cleanse you from your unrighteousness (1 John 1:9). The Bible says, do not give the accuser a "foothold" against you (see Ephesians 4:27). Demonic oppression does not affect our salvation. When we are born again, we are saved, but demonic oppression makes life less fun and enjoyable!

"Finally, my brethren, be strong in the Lord and in the power of His might. Put on the whole armor of God, that you may be able to stand against the wiles of the devil. For we do not wrestle against flesh and blood, but against principalities, against powers, against the rulers of the darkness of this age, against spiritual hosts of wickedness in the heavenly places. Therefore take up the whole armor of God, that you may be able to withstand in the evil day, and having done all, to stand. Stand therefore, having girded your waist with truth, having put on the breastplate of righteousness, and having shod your feet with the preparation of the gospel of peace; above all, taking the shield of faith with which you will be able to quench all the fiery darts of the wicked one." Ephesians 6:10-16 NKJV

The "flaming darts or arrows" in Ephesians 6:16 are lies that tempt us to sin. The enemy will tempt you where you are most vulnerable in your heart. We choose to sin when our emotional needs are unmet, so many times, instead of resisting the devil (see James 4:7) we partner with the flaming arrows through sin. In the example mentioned above with Wounded William, the "arrow" was to partner with sexual sin in the form of watching porn, or having sex with someone outside of marriage. William partnered with sin because he was looking for the needs of his heart to be met.

Generational Iniquities

Generational issues can also be a factor in a person's life. These are the sins that the generations before us committed. Unconfessed sins will manifest as anger, rage, rebellion, hate, unforgiveness and bitterness, adultery, lust, jealousy, victim mindset, etc. Demons will essentially be "passed down" to the next generation because the sins were never renounced or repented by anyone in the family line.

Pieter and I had many generational issues that needed to be addressed. Many cultures feel it is dishonorable to talk about sins in the family, however, the most honorable thing we can do is get healing so that we break the cycles of sin and bondage in our bloodline. I talked with my Mom extensively about the family history - not to cause shame, but to heal what was broken. I also really enjoyed our conversations and learned so much about my amazing mother. She is truly a hero who carried the weight for much of the family.

We have had the privilege of ministering deliverance to hundreds of couples. Recently, we ministered to a woman who had a childhood filled with abuse and trauma. Her parents were members of a cult and had performed occult rituals on the woman during childhood. Her parents were third generation cult members.

Miraculously, the woman had broken out of the cult and found Jesus. She was now in a high-level professional career. She had even gone through four years of ministry school at a well-known seminary, where they never taught about inner healing or deliverance.

She shared with us that she was "hearing voices," and "thought she was going crazy." She came across our website and reached out for us for help. Each person's story is unique, so based on what the woman told us, we knew we would need to spend three days with "Becky" in person. Becky flew to California to spend time with us in person, and we spent three full days with her.

We started by listening to Becky's story, and we asked Jesus to help us bring up issues in the soul that needed to be healed. We listened as Becky processed a lifetime of pain. During the deliverance Becky screamed a few times when the demons were leaving. We knew she was receiving freedom from the oppression that had left her feeling hopeless and bound. Jesus set her free! "For with shrieks, impure spirits came out of many, and many who were paralyzed or lame were healed." Acts 8:7 NIV. By the end of her three-day session, Becky was laughing and filled with the joy of the Holy Spirit. Jesus sets the captives free and restores all that was lost!

The Soul is the Filter to the Heart

"Beloved, I pray that you are prospering in every good way and that you continually enjoy good health, just as your soul is prospering." 3 John 1:2 NKJV

The soul is the filter to the heart, so unhealed soul issues will affect our peace and joy with others. Essentially, people can develop a "clogged heart filter." This clouded perception filters how we see God. For example, someone without an earthly father may view God the Father as distant and uncaring, based on their human father wounds. Their filter makes them feel abandoned by Father God. What we harbor in our souls inevitably spills out into our relationships. The goal in inner healing is removing filter-clogging soul toxins. As we relinquish lies, grudges, pride, and unhealthy bonds, our spiritual filter becomes unclogged. We begin seeing God, ourselves, and others through the lens of Christ-centered truth, not our soul's distortions.

"So above all, guard the affections of your heart, for they affect all that you are. Pay attention to the welfare of your innermost being, for from there flows the wellspring of life." Proverbs 4:23 TPT

Roots of Bitterness - Lies and Vows

"See to it that no one misses the revelation of God's grace. And make sure no one lives with a root of bitterness sprouting within them which will only cause trouble and poison the hearts of many." Hebrews 12:15 TPT

The lies Pieter and I believed as children turned into vows that followed us into adulthood - a vow drives a demonic agreement from the lies we believe. Here is an example: I am a terrible person for what I have done and unworthy of being forgiven (Lie); therefore, I will hide my heart so no one will ever find out what I have done (Vow). Vows are like a demonic whip that drives you until the vows are broken and replaced with the truth of God's word. The spirit realm feeds on agreement - whether truth or lies. Discovering whether we have made agreements based on truth or lies is the key to a major breakthrough.

"Don't you know that when you allow even a little lie into your heart, it can permeate your entire belief system?" Galatians 5:9 TPT

Vows are demonic when they are not grounded in the truth of God's word. "The truth will make you free" is not a metaphor, it is a spiritual reality. (see John 8:32). The lies Wounded William believed became a stronghold in William's mind. The wounds in our soul do not affect our salvation, but we will remain "double-minded" (doubting God), unless the wounds are healed, and replaced with the truth of God's word. James 1:8 says, "A double-minded man is unstable in all of his ways." The words "double-minded" in the original Greek actually means, "double-souled." Essentially, James 1:8 can be translated: "A double-souled man is unstable in all his ways."

Inner healing is the deepest form of soul healing- the healing of our mind, will, and emotions. The hidden wounds of our soul are brought out to the surface, healed, and brought to the cross. Thus, inner healing heals the deepest part of our soul - our inner man. Deliverance then clears out the demons. We systematically tear down strongholds, and replace them with the knowledge of God and His truth (2 Cor 10:3-5).

Removing the strongholds involves repenting and renouncing lies, vows, and sins resulting from our unbelief. We invite the Holy Spirit to reveal the truth for each situation where we have experienced pain or trauma. Inner (soul) healing finds the deepest lies and unbelief so that we can repent (change the way we think) and be cleansed from any unrighteousness.

"If we confess our sins he is faithful to cleanse us from all unrighteousness." 1 John 1:9 NKJV

Our negative emotions always have a source, and until the source is addressed and healed, the emotions associated with the experience will continue. Many have heard the word "triggered" a time or two. Triggers usually describe when we feel sad, angry, frustrated, hurt, or offended. Triggers are a warning light into a deeper spiritual reality, the condition of our soul. We often do not know why we feel "triggered" or upset, so we will try to stuff it down or ignore it. Ultimately, "triggered" moments are a warning light that something is not working properly. It's like a "check under the hood of the car" warning light. We can ignore the warning light, but eventually, the car will break down if the issue is not addressed.

When our heart and soul are hurting, we will eventually react to the pain we are feeling. Reactions can vary, but the central issue is always an issue of the heart and soul. Jesus promised when he left that the Holy Spirit would teach us and lead us into all truth (John 14:26). When we go through life with an unhealed soul, we will put walls up to guard our heart against experiencing more pain. The walls of self-protection we put up can ultimately prevent us from connecting deeply with others or with God. Because the heart is the filter to the soul, the unresolved issues in our soul (wounds) are the filter to our beliefs.

Pieter's Healing Journey

Through inner healing, Pieter discovered that he used pornography and lust to escape the pain he was feeling in his heart and soul (Read, Silently Broken, Loudly Restored, for Pieter's full redemption story). A demonic stronghold was established in Pieter's life as a young boy when he was only seven years old. Pieter was exposed to pornography at a birthday party. The boys at the party liked the pornographic video that the hosting Dad had rented for the young boys, so Pieter decided that this is what boys did to be "cool." Therefore, whenever emotional stress set in, Pieter's response was to use pornography to "numb out" the emotional pain in his heart. This later turned into looking to women for physical affirmation.

Pieter discovered that pornography was not the root, but sin he used to deal with the pain in his heart (which was a wound in the soul). Pieter has often said that pornography was not the problem in his life, It was the solution. Pieter didn't realize this until he was able to find the root of this pain. This pain later became a bitter root of pride when Pieter became an adult (see the chapter on Pride for the full description of pride). When Pieter was a little boy, his mother was an alcoholic, and although she was a good mom, when she would drink she often forgot to pick him up from school and other events. He was often left for hours. His home was filled with yelling and fighting between his parents because of the drinking.

Pieter felt responsible for the fighting in his home because of the accusatory nature of the fighting between his parents, so he would hide in his room. Pieter's father traveled for work and was often gone, leaving Pieter alone with his little sister and his mother. Pieter had a great father but as a child, he experienced both a geographic and relational absence of his father and mother. Pieter was left without anyone to care for his heart, and he believed the lie that this was all his fault and made the vow to control all circumstances in his life so that he would never have to experience this pain again.

Pieter went into an encounter with Jesus during his inner healing and deliverance session and discovered the lie and vow he made as a child; "I am not worthy of being pursued and can't count on anyone to be with me when I need it, so I will have to take care of my happiness myself." Finally, Pieter could see the truth over the pain in his heart. Pieter had the revelation of the lie that he believed, which had become a demonic stronghold. The stronghold was the result of abandonment as a child. In his inner healing session, the demonic stronghold abandonment was replaced with a heavenly stronghold of protection, which was rooted in the truth of God's word. The demons then had no legal right to harass Pieter, and were forced to l eave! Pieter had to go through the inner healing process to identify the lie he believed about himself because you cannot put truth over the pain in your heart and soul - an encounter with Jesus will change everything!

Melinda's Healing Journey

Forgiving Pieter was the most important aspect of my healing journey, but I also needed to forgive myself. I was holding on to so many lies about who God said I was. The lies were keeping me stuck in a cycle of shame. Shame is the enemy of our spiritual growth and it was hindering me from connecting with Pieter the way I truly desired. No matter how many times I tried to get close to Pieter by opening my heart, I would always choose to shut down and go into hiding. Hiding for me looked like silence. Pieter would ask me what was wrong and I would say, "Nothing, I am fine." Well, I was not fine, and it wasn't his fault at all. The problem was I was holding on to pain that I needed to address with Jesus.

The Lord asked me one day, "Melinda, are you ready to deal with that pain?" Although we had gone through inner healing and deliverance, I was still working on healing my soul completely. Together with the Holy Spirit, I was able to uncover the lies I was subconsciously believing about myself and God. The lies were causing me to feel shame from what I had done in the past. Until I was ready to forgive myself and hand that pain over to Jesus, I could not be healed.

Fighting with the Right Weapon - Love

Love is how we win the battle with the enemy. Loving others can happen when we pursue healing for ourselves. Pieter and I are now more connected than we ever thought possible. The events of our past are now far behind us because we have pursued the healing of our souls. Jesus said, "Come to me, all of you who are weary and carry heavy burdens, and I will give you rest. Take my yoke upon you. Let me teach you, because I am humble and gentle at heart, and you will find rest for your souls. For my yoke is easy to bear, and the burden I give you is light." Matthew 11:28-30 NLT.

Conclusion

No matter what has happened in your past or what emotions you are feeling as you read this chapter, your identity is rooted in Christ. Your birth and purpose on earth is unique and extraordinarily special. Whether you identify with what Pieter and I went through, or the story of "Wounded William" or "Becky," nothing is beyond the healing, restorative power of Jesus. It is in His mercy that sometimes roots, strongholds, and triggers are revealed. I know that God is doing a big work in your life because you mean everything to Him. The heart of the Father is one of unconditional love for you and He is so proud of you!

Chapter 5

Tearing Down Strongholds in the Mind

"Be transformed by the renewing of the mind."

Romans 12:2 NKJV

When I found out Pieter had been unfaithful, I battled so much doubt and unbelief that our marriage would be restored. Even though I had heard the audible voice of God, and Pieter had a vision of Jesus, the enemy came in with every arrow he possibly could during this season to plant seeds of doubt, insecurity, and unbelief. One day in particular, I was driving in my car, and I had a random thought, *"Are you sure God really said he was going to restore your marriage?"* It wasn't a loud booming voice, but it was just a thought that could have passed as my own thought. The greatest revelation we can have as believers is we can choose what we believe.

The world and the enemy were screaming at me during this season, "Get a divorce! He will just do it again!" The world can be less than hope-filled when it comes to seeing people restored and living in redemption, but something inside of me held onto the truth that God was faithful and I could count on Him to fulfill what He had promised.

Believing the truth was not easy. There were many painful days when I would spend hours in my secret place with the Lord. I would pray and seek Him and His wisdom. Many days, I did not want to leave the secret place because facing the world was so discouraging. I was never suicidal or depressed, but I struggled with anxiety, doubt, and fear. Thoughts would run through my head, such as, "What if people found out? What if our kids found out? What if Pieter loses his job? What if…."

The Battle is Always for the Mind

The mind is where the enemy launches his heaviest attacks. Strongholds are formed when we partner with the lies of the enemy. **Strongholds are any belief system that opposes the truth in the Word of God.** Most of the time, strongholds are formed during childhood, when we are the most vulnerable and not equipped to fight effectively in a spiritual battle. It is difficult to "resist the devil" as a child when you do not understand spiritual warfare. Children should be taught to identify lies and replace them with the truth at a young age. Otherwise, they will be susceptible to attacks and need the proper defense system to fight the enemy's lies.

Pieter and I grew up in homes that were very different. Although our parents loved us deeply, we were not taught truths about spiritual warfare. The lies we believed as children followed us into adulthood, such as, "I am not smart. I will never measure up. I have to perform for love. I am unworthy. God did not protect me, so I cannot trust Him." Lies, when believed, become strongholds. As we go through life and experience more pain, the strongholds are solidified. The lies we believe become the definition of a stronghold, which is a fortress.

Fortresses are not easily taken down, and they have multiple defense systems in place to protect themselves. Fortresses are built over time; one lie on top of the other.

"As a man thinks in his heart, so is he…" Proverbs 23:7 NKJV

Tearing Down Strongholds

Vows are often attached to lies, and they can be one of the defense systems within a stronghold. Vows are an agreement based upon a lie. One of the lies and vows I had partnered with was, "I will never measure up. Therefore, I will strive as hard as I can to earn love. God did not protect me. Therefore, I won't fully trust Him." Lies and vows form our thought patterns. Those thought patterns look for proof of what they believe. When we go through life and experience more pain, the lies and vows are reinforced. This is how strongholds are formed.

Not all strongholds are evil; strongholds can be built upon truth or lies. Strongholds of truth are built on the truth of God's word manifest as the fruit of the Spirit, "Love, joy, peace, kindness, goodness, faithfulness, gentleness and self-control (Galatians 5:22)." Strongholds built on lies manifest demonically in the form of rejection, abandonment, fear, anger, pride, anxiety, depression, rebellion, victim mindset, and the list goes on.

Strongholds form in our soul, which is our mind, will, and emotions. There are two types of strongholds: Heavenly Strongholds based on the truth of God's Word, and Demonic Strongholds, based on lies from the enemy. Strongholds can be formed by words spoken over us by those closest to us in the form of word curses. Lies spoken over us are powerful and can cause pain and trauma if they are not torn down with the truth of God's word.

"Death and life are in the power of the tongue, And those who love it will eat its fruit." Proverbs 18:21 NKJV

Words of death, "word curses," spoken over us as children or adults, must be replaced by words of life. Words of life are the truth that comes only from the word of God.

"For the word of God is alive and active. Sharper than any double-edged sword, it penetrates even to dividing soul and spirit, joints and marrow; it judges the thoughts and attitudes of the heart." Hebrews 4:12 NIV

Tearing down strongholds is a violent act where we refuse to believe the lies spoken over our lives. The important thing to remember is to not be passive as you renew your mind. Tearing down strongholds is an active activity. We must choose to aggressively oppose anything that contradicts the knowledge of God. "Casting down" means: "to take down, with the use of violent force: to throw down, cast down, to pull down, or demolish (Strongs G2506)."

Practically, believers can pray to have strongholds revealed by the Holy Spirit. God is so faithful, and He will reveal thought patterns that are holding you back from stepping into the abundant life (see John 10:10). Below is a series of steps to identify how demonic strongholds are formed and how to tear them down. It is wisdom to bring a trusted friend or mentor into the process of tearing down strongholds or identifying lies. Bringing a trusted community into my process is what helped me the most. Pray and ask the Holy Spirit to reveal areas where strongholds may have been formed in your life.

Steps To Identify Strongholds and Tear Them Down:

Cycle of Strongholds

(Christa Smith, Healing and Deliverance Masterclass)

1. The enemy will tell you a lie. A lie is anything that contradicts the truth of God's word.
2. Once a lie is believed, it becomes deception
3. That deception becomes a mindset
4. That deception leads to feelings
5. Those feelings lead to actions
6. Those actions become habits
7. Those habits become cycles

Cycle of Tearing Down Strongholds:
(Pieter and Melinda Lagaay, Arise & Shine Ministries)

1. Identify the lie from the enemy.
2. Identify the vow (demonic agreement).
3. Ask the Holy Spirit to show you where the lie and vow came from (the root of the stronghold).
4. Find the truth in the Word of God.
5. Repent (agree to turn to truth) and renounce (break agreement with the sin or thought pattern).
6. Forgive and Bless the person who cursed you or hurt you (if applicable).
7. Turn the truth into a declaration and it will become a new, Godly stronghold based on the truth of God's word.

Healing the Soul

Acts 10:38 says, "how God anointed Jesus of Nazareth with the Holy Spirit and with power, who went about doing good and healing all who were oppressed by the devil, for God was with Him." Acts 10:38 NKJV. The word "power" is the word "dunamis," and it means strength, power, ability, power for performing miracles and excellence of the soul." Our soul (our mind, will, and emotions) is where the supernatural healing power of God sets us free.

"Beloved, I pray that you may prosper in all things and be in health, just as your soul prospers." 3 John 1:2 NKJV

The Holy Spirit supernaturally helps us become transformed in our soul. Healing the soul is critical because **the soul is the filter to the heart.**

"As a man thinks in his heart so is he…" Proverbs 23:7 NKJV

Years ago, I had a conversation with someone I wasn't looking forward to. On the way to have the conversation, I rehearsed the worst-case scenario in my mind. I would think, "This conversation is going to be hard." and I would actually imagine a poor outcome. The worst part was that I was prophesying lies over myself and partnering with a demonic agenda, which was to destroy a healthy relationship. I had a stronghold of fear of man, which manifested in my thoughts.

To get free, I had to identify the lie I was believing. The lie was rooted in a vow of self-protection. "I have been hurt before in relationships, so I will have to protect myself in this conversation so I don't get hurt." I have learned to recognize strongholds by the thoughts they leave behind. One of the ways to recognize if you are struggling with strongholds is to pay attention to your thought life. What are you meditating on or thinking about? Do you imagine the best-case scenario or the worst-case scenario?

Once lies and vows are identified and replaced with truth, we can begin to meditate on truth, and form a new heavenly stronghold based on God's word. Since I have started intentionally replacing demonic strongholds with heavenly strongholds, I am far happier and filled with more peace and joy. I have learned to speak blessings out loud over my future conversations, and I imagine a positive outcome. I use my sanctified imagination to visualize the best-case scenario for myself and the other person.

Flaming Arrows from the Enemy

One time, I was at church during worship and thought, "That person standing in front of you didn't say hello when you walked into the building today. They probably don't like you." The lie was an attempt by the enemy to get me to partner with the thought. Instead of agreeing with a demonic agenda, which aimed to cause division between myself and my sister in Christ, I had to choose to cast the thought down.

The worship music played loudly, so I said, "My friend loves me, and I love her! I bless our friendship in Jesus' name! I forgive her if she has spoken any evil against me." Just then, something powerful happened. Out of nowhere, my friend turned around, walked over to me and said, "Hi! I forgot to say hi to you when you came in!" Then, she embraced me with a hug.

The Power of Agreement

The agreements we make in our minds are incredibly powerful in the realm of the spirit, and those agreements will manifest in the natural realm. We can bless those around us or curse them with our thoughts and words. "When someone curses you, bless that person in return. When you are mistreated and harassed by others, accept it as your mission to pray for them." Luke 6:28 TPT. The Apostle Paul teaches us to tear down every thought that exalts itself against the knowledge of God (see 2 Corinthians 10: 4-5). Casting down thoughts is an intentional act to choose to think about higher things and believe the best of others. **One of the most significant revelations we can have as believers is that we can choose what we believe.** Thanks to Steve and Wendy Backlund for imparting this profound revelation to me and many others.

"Finally, brethren, whatever things are true, whatever things are noble, whatever things are just, whatever things are pure, whatever things are lovely, whatever things are of good report, if there is any virtue and if there is anything praiseworthy—meditate on these things." Philippians 4:8 NKJV

The Bible uses the word blessing over 200 times! Blessings break the power of curses. When we intentionally forgive and bless those around us (even our enemies) and pray for those who curse us, we destroy the works of the enemy by taking our thoughts captive into the obedience of Christ. Blessings are far more powerful than curses.

"When someone curses you, bless that person in return. When you are mistreated and harassed by others, accept it as your mission to pray for them." Luke 6:28 TPT

Our Sanctified Imagination

One of the areas of belief I worked out was in the area of belief around my marriage. My thoughts were very revealing because I rarely imagined the best-case scenario. I was actually meditating on lies! It's no wonder I was stressed out, riddled with anxiety, and in self-protection mode every time I had a conversation with Pieter. My walls of self-protection were up because I had already imagined the worst-case scenario! I was giving the devil a lot to work with instead of meditating on the truth and having high beliefs for our future conversations.

I believe that heavenly understanding is in fact often the fruit from meditation on God's truth about His character and my identity. I love that one of the translations for the Hebrew word meditation, *hagah*, is imagination. So, Psalms 49.3 "My mouth shall speak wisdom, And the meditation of my heart shall give understanding" could be paraphrased to mean "when my heart *imagines* the truth of God I give understanding". What I meditate on, frames how I understand God, myself, and people.

For example, Pieter would come home, and I would feel frustrated with him because of the conversation I had imagined. He was already doomed because I was believing lies and rehearsing those lies before he even walked through the front door! I was already upset that he had not taken the garbage out or done something around the house. The truth is we cannot find our fulfillment in what our spouse does or does not do. Our fulfillment must be found in our relationship with Jesus. When we meditate on Him and His truth, all of those other small things seem to matter less and less. The small things are minuscule compared to the love of Christ.

Seeking Heart Connection

The goal in marriage is always heart connection. Every conversation should be aimed at connecting with our spouse rather than seeking a desired outcome for ourselves, but this can be very difficult if we are meditating on lies. For this reason, the more emotionally healed and healthy we are in our mindsets and beliefs, the better our marriages and relationships will be. God's will is that we have an abundant life and that we are healed spirit, soul, and body.

"Now may the God of peace Himself sanctify you completely; and may your whole spirit, soul, and body be preserved blameless at the coming of our Lord Jesus Christ." I Thessalonians 5:23 NKJV

The Holy Spirit will guide you through the process of mind renewal. Take one lie at a time, and focus on finding the truth, and meditating on the truth. The grace of God will get you through to the other side. Grace is God's divine enablement or empowerment. He is the one who sanctifies us. Our job is to partner with what the Lord is saying and make that our truth.

"'Not by might nor by power, but by My Spirit,' Says the Lord of hosts." Zechariah 4:6 b NKJV

Prayer

Father, I thank you that you are taking me on an exciting journey of mind renewal. I thank you that it is not by might, or power, but by Your Spirit that I will be led into all truth. I thank you that you have given me a sound mind. Thank you that you are with me and will never leave me or forsake me. With you, all things are possible! Thank you for taking me on this journey. I ask for wisdom, guidance, and to know you more. I pour the blood of Jesus over my body, soul, and spirit, and ask for heavenly angels to protect me and surround me as I go through the mind renewal journey. I pray this in Jesus' name. Amen.

SECTION TWO

Supernatural Prayers for Deliverance

Chapter 6

Breaking Generational Curses - The Power of a Blessing

"I will make you a great nation; I will bless you And make your name great; And you shall be a blessing. I will bless those who bless you, And I will curse him who curses you; And in you all the families of the earth shall be blessed."

Genesis 12:2-3 NKJV

Generational curses are visible in the natural realm as chaos and destruction in a person's life. Generational curses are passed down the bloodline until someone breaks the curse through the blood of Jesus. Once a curse is broken, the person can receive the blessing the Lord intended for them and their family line. Generations will benefit from a curse being broken. Generational lines in families are being robbed of the blessings from God simply because many people do not understand how to break agreements with curses by the power of the blood of Jesus.

Honoring God's spiritual laws prevents the enemy from having a foothold in our lives through a curse. We are not under the old covenant law. However, there are still spiritual principles to follow. When we follow God's spiritual principles, we are protected from the destruction of the enemy. God's laws and principles protect us so that we can live the abundant life Jesus came to give (see John 10:10).

When we violate one of God's spiritual laws or principles, we give the enemy a foothold, and allow a potential curse into our bloodline. Dishonoring your parents gives the enemy access to your life. Even parents who have mistreated us can still be honored. Although sometimes it is unhealthy to keep a relationship with our parents, this does not give us permission to dishonor our parents through our thoughts or words. We are required to forgive our parents and release them to Jesus, regardless of their actions towards us.

Here are some examples of some of God's spiritual laws or spiritual principles:

- Honor your mother and father (Matthew 19:19)
- Forgiving others (Matthew 6:14 - 15, Hebrews 12:15)
- Loving God and our neighbors (Mark 12:30 - 31)
- Blessing those who curse us (Luke 6:28)
- Faith - never doubting God's promises or His word (James 1:6 - 8, Hebrews 11:6)
- Do not fear (Isaiah 41:10)
- Not judging others (Matthew 7:1 - 2)
- Being a cheerful giver and tithing (2 Corinthians 9:6 - 8)
- Etc.

The Power of the Blood of Jesus

The good news is, "When we confess our sins he is faithful and just to cleanse us from all unrighteousness." (1 John 1:9). All means ALL - the power of the blood of Jesus can free you from all curses the enemy has placed upon your life (see prayer to break generational curses at the end of this chapter). Repenting for the sins of your ancestors is called "Identificational Repentance." Examples of Identificational Repentance can be found in Nehemiah 1:6-9, and 1 Corinthians 7:14. Confessing a curse involves repenting and renouncing the sin you committed or the sin that your ancestors committed.

Divorce was a generational curse over my family line, and poverty. Money came in and went out as though there was an invisible hole in our bank accounts. Our family did not tithe. Therefore, we were violating one of God's spiritual principles of tithing and being a cheerful giver. Divorce was also common, and so was infidelity. Generations of women in our family line had husbands who had been unfaithful. Our family had violated one of God's spiritual laws and no one had repented for the sins that were committed. Word curses can also affect the level of freedom we will walk in. We give word curses power when we agree with the lies spoken over us.

Seven Signs you are living under a Curse

(from Derek Prince's book, Blessing or Curse)

1. Mental and Emotional Breakdown
2. Repeated or chronic sickness (especially if hereditary)
3. Barrenness, a tendency to miscarry, or related female problems
4. Breakdown of marriage and family alienation
5. Continuing financial insufficiency
6. Being accident prone
7. A history of suicides and unnatural and untimely death

Blessing Focused

Wherever there is a generational curse in a person's life, there is a generational blessing that has been withheld because of the curse. In the Old Testament, people would lie and cheat to receive the blessing from the father. Blessings were so powerful that Jacob took his mother's advice to lie to his Father to receive his brother Esau's blessing (see Genesis 27). Blessings were understood as being powerful in the Old Testament. The question we must ask is, how much more powerful is a blessing under the new covenant?

I used to be curse-focused, but the Lord started speaking to me about being blessing-focused. Blessings are far more powerful than curses, especially under the new covenant. For this reason, the enemy works overtime to withhold blessings from us. It is really our lack of awareness in the spiritual realm that causes blessings to be withheld. The blood of Jesus can cancel out any curse in any bloodline.

Blessings Fulfilled

I am starting to live in the promises and blessings the Lord spoke many years ago in a season when my marriage was falling apart. He has not only restored my marriage, but He has given me joy, peace, and deep fulfillment in Jesus. God is faithful, and when we attach faith to His promises, truly, anything is possible. Many years ago I wrote in my journal, "Lord, Do whatever it takes to bring Pieter to you." However, I only started to see promises manifest in my life once the curses were broken and replaced with blessings instead.

"Blessed (happy to be envied) is she who believed that there would be fulfillment of the things that were spoken to her from the Lord." Luke 1:45 AMPC

The Wilderness Season

The season of waiting for promises and blessings to be fulfilled can be long. Waiting may feel passive in the natural, but it is very active in the Spirit. Psalm 27:14 speaks about how we are to navigate these seasons of waiting. "Wait and hope for and expect the Lord; be brave and of good courage and let your heart be stout and enduring. Yes, wait for and hope for and expect the Lord." The word wait in Hebrew is *kawvaw*. It translates more directly to, eagerly expecting. When we are waiting for the fulfillment of God's promises we are being invited to eagerly expect God to deliver!

Pieter and I were in ministry school for three years. Although we had an amazing experience at school (we are forever grateful for our time at Bethel Supernatural School of Ministry), the days were sometimes long and emotional. There were many days I would have to remind myself of who I was and what God had promised. Pieter and I had no idea what was ahead of us during our time in school. We had no "backup plan" for our lives. We were both in our forties, and had given it all up to come to school and follow the call of God in our lives. Sometimes, when we are in the midst of following God, it is easy to lose focus. All we knew for sure is that God had promised to bless us.

During ministry school, we started receiving prophetic words about the future and areas where God wanted to bless us. I am so thankful for the gift of prophecy in the church. It keeps the compass of our hearts focused on the most important thing - Jesus. Prophecy reminds us of God's love, faithfulness, and promises to us. Prophetic words guide, encourage, comfort, and keep us focused on Jesus so that we do not lose heart and give up.

"And let us not grow weary while doing good, for in due season we shall reap if we do not lose heart." Galatians 6:9 NKJV

The Power of Prophecy

The prophetic words we started receiving were exciting and encouraged us to keep going. The prophecies were like pieces of a "blessing puzzle" that God was revealing to us over time. The Bible says that we all "prophesy in part (see 1 Corinthians 13:9)." God was revealing His heart and plans for us during our time in ministry school in pieces. We were so grateful to the faithful saints who stepped out to reveal the Father's plans for us through prophecy.

During school, I received a prophetic word with Pieter on the last day of school from one of the revival group pastors at Bethel. He said that Pieter and I were builders and that God would give us places to build for His Kingdom. Pieter and I also received prophetic words about a medical device invention. Another Bethel pastor walked up to Pieter and said, "I am hearing ' Bezalel' and 'Patent.'" Bezalel is the name of Pieter's medical device company, and when we received the word, we had just put thousands of dollars of our own money towards the patent!

One of the areas in which the enemy likes to withhold blessings from believers is in the area of finance. Pieter and I started receiving prophetic words that financial blessings were in our bloodline. We had repented for the curse of poverty, and since then, we have started to see financial blessings increase.

One night, Pieter and I prayed that God would give us one more confirmation to move forward with the medical company, Bezalel. We went to church the next morning, and the pastor taking the offering stopped and said, "Someone in here is inventing a device, and God says to do it!" We were shocked and knew the prophetic word was for us! We approached the pastor after the service, and without hesitation, she started prophesying about God sending finances and investors to fulfill the dream of Bezalel. We had not told her we needed any finances. She prophesied blessings over us. These are just a few examples of how God spoke directly to us about blessings through prophecy, and we are so grateful.

Dreams in the Night

God also revealed His plans for us through dreams in the night. While living in the Bay Area, I started having more dreams. I went to sleep one night and had a dream that I was flying. A huge angel was holding me and we were flying together through the night sky. I could see stars everywhere.

I looked down and could see a city surrounded by sand. I immediately knew it was Israel. A crystal clear river ran through the city, and homes surrounded the river.

The Lord started speaking to me about Israel representing the nations. The Lord told me I was called to minister to the nations. Since this dream, we have ministered to people from all nations who came up to Redding to attend ministry school. God has brought the nations to us! We have ministered to individuals from India, Brazil, Germany, and Canada, and we know this is just the beginning. God truly "Watches over His word to perform it (see Jeremiah 1:12)." Our daughter is attending her second year of ministry school as I write this. We had many prophetic words that she would be saved and attend ministry school. God truly blessed us beyond what we could ask, think or imagine, and He will do the same for you.

Can curses affect my physical health?

The short answer is, yes. Pieter and I ministered to a man who had Freemason in his bloodline. His Father was heavily involved in the secret society and had made several agreements and vows. We took the man through prayer to break agreement with the curses concerning himself and his bloodline. Freemasons invoke physical and mental curses on the family line for anyone who leaves the secret society or violates its protocol.

Before his prayer session with us, the man had been in and out of the hospital for multiple complications that would not heal. He had spent a fortune on doctors and had multiple diagnoses and no solutions to his health issues. The man was very healthy and in his mid-thirties, so the complications were not expected.

We went through the prayer to break agreement with the curses, and the man was completely healed in church healing rooms the following weekend from all of his infirmities!

He was completely set free and is still free of all sickness today. The curse was replaced with the promise of physical health. The curse was replaced with a blessing!

Unforgiveness can also hinder our physical healing. I have seen people release forgiveness and become physically healed as a result of their choice to release the person to Jesus.

Below is a prayer to break any curse over your life and replace the curse with a blessing:

Father, thank you for the many blessings in my bloodline. I thank you for your goodness and mercy concerning me and my family line. In the name of Jesus I renounce (say the sin you committed or the generations before you) _____ . I repent for this sin (change the way I think and break agreement with sin) and break agreement with it in Jesus' name. I come to you humbly and ask that you forgive me and the generations before me, back to Adam, for the sins committed in my bloodline. I now cancel the curse over my family line and break its power with the blood of Jesus. I break every demonic soul-tie and agreement that was made concerning this sin and violation of Your spiritual laws. Thank you for your forgiveness and blessings. I now receive the blessing you have for my family line and look forward to seeing it manifest in the natural realm.

Chapter 7

The Power of Forgiveness

"Put on then, as God's chosen ones, holy and beloved, compassionate hearts, kindness, humility, meekness, and patience, bearing with one another and, if one has a complaint against another, forgiving each other; as the Lord has forgiven you, so you also must forgive."

Colossians 3:12-13 ESV

I tried to forgive Pieter so many times before we went through our inner healing and deliverance session, but the feelings of anger, pain, and abandonment would continually resurface. The reason is because I had no understanding of what true forgiveness was, or how to walk myself through the process of forgiving Pieter. I wanted so desperately to be free of the memories associated with the pain, but each time I tried, I felt frustrated and discouraged. I was trying to forgive Pieter in my own strength and without processing the pain with Jesus.

Forgiveness starts with understanding our story. Our story makes up who we are and why our hearts react the way they do when we experience pain. When I was ten years old I was bullied at school, and the situation became so severe that I did not want to go to school in the morning. I would cry and beg my mom not to make me go because I dreaded the group of girls that awaited me every morning. My Mom advocated for me, but regardless of her efforts, the bullying continued.

I was deeply hurt by these events and as a result, I formed a belief that something was wrong with me. I also believed the lie that I was abandoned, alone, and rejected. I also believed I was the only one experiencing this sort of pain.

The bullying happened when I was nine years old, right in the middle of my parent's divorce. The lie that I could not trust anyone became a demonic stronghold in the form of a vow, and as a result, I closed my heart off to deep friendships to protect myself from getting hurt. I also became bitter and unforgiving towards certain individuals.

I had no idea the lie I had believed as a child was reinforced when I learned that Pieter was addicted to sex and pornography. Once again, I believed I was not good enough, alone, abandoned, and that something was wrong with me. During my inner healing and deliverance session, the Holy Spirit revealed that I had believed many lies and made several vows. "I am alone, so I will have to take care of myself" is just one example of the many lies and vows I had made in my heart.

Getting to the Root

Forgiveness involves getting to the root of the pain and discovering the stronghold (lie and vow) associated with the pain. Knowing your story really means gaining a perception through revelation. When we know our story we receive a revelation of how God perceives our life in truth rather than how we perceive it based on lies and strongholds. It is through our humility and surrender to go back into the story of our life that God shows up and says "Hey Melinda, this is how I perceive your life story". Without this revelation, we will walk in partial freedom because what we are perceiving from our life is not based on the truth of what God perceives.

Demons love to lie for the purpose of perverting how we perceive ourselves and our story. This demonic perversion of our identity stems from a deception of how God perceives ourselves and our story by reminding us of historical pain such as rejection, anger, and bitterness. Finding the root of the pain in your story through the revelation of knowing how God perceives your identity and story is what leads to true freedom.

Forgiving Yourself

Forgiveness sometimes involves forgiving ourselves. Pieter worked hard to overcome this stronghold. Albeit there was a level of surrender to admit he had a problem and was not in control of it, another layer involved surrendering his mind to believe that he was worthy of forgiveness despite what he had done and caused.

After the truth of what Pieter had done was revealed, Pieter went to counseling several days a week and began serving at the church, men's group, and with local halfway recovery homes to encourage and pray for men. Amid this, Pieter developed a theology of a martyr mindset. Pieter believed that his forgiveness was conditional on serving others. This meant that Pieter believed the new covenant in part. For example, Pieter believed the scripture which says "He who believes and is baptized will be saved, but he who does not believe will be condemned." Mark 16:16, but when he read other scripture like , "If we confess our sins, he is faithful and just to forgive us our sins, and to cleanse us from all unrighteousness. " 1 John 1:9

The stronghold preventing Pieter from fully believing he was worthy of receiving the new covenant was rooted in the lie that love was always conditional on some accomplishment or achievement. So if forgiveness from the Father was rooted in love, then there had to be a condition of performance attached. This martyr mindset is why Pieter relentlessly served. Pieter believed he was not worthy of forgiveness and that if he truly forgave himself, he would backslide. So the vow Pieter made after he was saved was, "I will never stop serving the church to ensure my forgiveness is not revoked."

When Pieter went through inner healing and deliverance, he had an encounter with Jesus when he was five years old that revealed the truth. In this encounter, Pieter was alone in his room, sitting on his bed. He could hear his parents screaming at each other. His mother was drunk, and his dad was frustrated. In this encounter, Jesus was sitting next to Pieter on his bed. Pieter asked Jesus what truth He would speak into Pieter's heart about what he believed about Pieter in this situation.

Jesus put his arm around Pieter and told him that his parents fighting and his mom's alcoholism was not his fault or responsibility to control. Jesus told Pieter that He was proud of him for being who he was and that Pieter was a great kid. Jesus told Pieter that academic and professional success, controlling happiness in the family, and holding onto the pain and shame was not what Pieter needed to do to be forgiven. Jesus whispered to Pieter, "You are worthy of forgiveness, and I trust you. I will always be with you, and you don't have to perform for love or forgiveness." The revelation of this truth broke off strongholds of false humility, pornography, lust, pride, and bitterness toward himself.

The Bitter Soul

Sinning opens doors for the enemy to occupy our souls, and bitterness is the result of prolonged unforgiveness. I hear the statement, "You have no idea what they did to me" all the time. I understand that forgiveness is hard, because I have forgiven for really hard things, but what is even harder is going through life with a bitter heart. Ultimately, we can choose to step into freedom, by releasing the person for Jesus to deal with, or we can hold on to bitterness, thus, giving the demons permission to camp out on our souls.

"Exercise foresight and be on the watch to look (after one another), to see what no one falls back from and fails to secure God's grace (His unmerited favor and spiritual blessing), in order that no **root of resentment (rancor, bitterness or hatred)** shoots forth and causes trouble and bitter torment, and the many become contaminated and defiled by it;" Hebrews 12:15 NKJV (emphasis mine)

Jesus tells us, "For if you forgive men their trespasses, your Heavenly Father will also forgive you. But if you do not forgive men their trespasses, neither will your Father forgive your trespasses." Matthew 6:14-15. Jesus had a conversation with the Apostle Peter about forgiveness. Peter himself was no doubt struggling to forgive, as we all do at times when we have been wrongfully hurt or taken advantage of by those closest to us. Peter asks Jesus, "Lord, how often shall my brother sin against me, and I forgive him? Up to seven times?" Jesus said to him, "I do not say to you up to seven times, but up to seventy times seven (Matthew 18:21-22). After Jesus told Peter to forgive as many times as it takes, he went on to share a parable. This story is a striking picture of what happens when we choose not to forgive.

"Therefore the kingdom of heaven is like a certain king who wanted to settle accounts with his servants. And when he had begun to settle accounts, one was brought to him who owed him ten thousand talents (a large sum of money). But as he was not able to pay, his master commanded that he be sold with his wife and children and all that he had and that payment be made. The servant therefore fell down before him saying, 'Master, have patience with me, and I will pay you all.' Then the master of that servant was moved with compassion, released him, and forgave him his debt. But that servant went out and found one of his fellow servants who owed him a hundred denarii; and he laid hands on him and took him by the throat, saying, 'Pay me what you owe!' So his fellow servant fell down at his feet and begged him, saying, "Have patience with me, and I will pay you all." And he would not, but went and threw him in prison till he should pay the debt. So when his fellow servants saw what he had done, they were very grieved, and came and told their master all that had been done. Then his master, after he had called him, said to him, ' You wicked servant! I forgave you all that debt because you begged me, Should you not also have had compassion on your fellow servant, just as I had pity on you? And his master was angry and delivered him to the torturers until he could pay back all that was due to him. "So my Heavenly Father also will do to you if each of you, from his heart, does not forgive his brother his trespasses." Matthew 18:23-35 NKJV

This parable demonstrates the spiritual consequences of unforgiveness and bitterness. We are literally released to the torturers - these are demons. Forgiveness is a choice we make each day, and the power to release ourselves and others from the demonic realm is in our hands. When we choose to forgive as our Heavenly Father has forgiven us, we take back that ground the enemy has taken in our souls, and we replace the lies about that situation with the truth. Unforgiveness is the bait of Satan, but forgiveness is a powerful weapon that contains the power to set the believer free.

Forgiving does not mean we continue to allow the person who hurt us to mistreat us. Many times we have forgiven after ending an unhealthy relationship. Our choice to forgive is not based on the other person's actions or response towards us. We make a choice to release the person to Jesus, regardless of their actions so that we will not grow a bitter root (demonic stronghold) in our soul. When we release the person to Jesus, we are repenting (changing our minds), and replacing lies and renouncing vows and replacing them with the truth. When we do this, heaven invades, and we gain back ground we mistakenly gave to the enemy. The power to be free from bitterness is truly in our hands, but requires a relinquishment of our deserved entitlement to be right about what we are feeling.

I had to choose to forgive Pieter for infidelity and lying. I understand that forgiveness is hard, but we know the spiritual consequences of unforgiveness are far worse. Even if my marriage was not restored, I would still forgive Pieter because of the demonic consequences for him and for me.

The Choice to Forgive

I have learned that whether the relationship is restored or not, I will still choose to walk in forgiveness. Forgiveness is simply not a choice if we want to stay free from oppression in our souls. Pieter and I live our lives in a constant state of forgiveness, and we refuse to let bitterness take root. We do this because we understand that unforgiveness will ultimately have negative spiritual consequences that will (literally) torment us if we refuse to hold onto the offense. We take this so seriously that we refuse to go to bed until everything is settled in our hearts. Forgiveness is a choice that we choose to walk in every day, and is not optional if we want to live victoriously.

"For you, Lord are king and ready to forgive, abounding in faithful love to all who call on you." Psalm 86:5 NKJV

Forgiveness is The Key to Heart Connection

One of the reasons relationships struggle is that people are looking for their emotional needs to be fulfilled through other people. I was just like this, until I realized a powerful key to connecting deeply with Pieter and others. Whenever I was hurting from something Pieter did or said, I would come to him and expect him to meet my emotional needs. I was focused on one thing - my pain and making sure Pieter knew how hurt I was. When our hearts are not healed, we will have walls of self-protection up, even in our closest relationships. I did this for most of my life. My heart was a fortress of walls. I was guarding my heart, or at least that is what I thought I was doing. When in reality, I was refusing to be vulnerable because I was protecting my heart from experiencing more pain.

Our goal in our relationships must be heart connection. When we make connection the priority, we are focusing on the health of the relationship and not the fulfillment of our own personal needs to be met through that person. Love and deep heart connection are birthed from intentionally focusing on the quality of our connection. Loving Pieter means I have to focus on what our relationship needs in order to stay connected. Even when there have been times when Pieter said something that hurt me, I must come into that conversation after I have forgiven Pieter with a heart that is postured towards connection, not focused on my need to tell Pieter how wrong he was and how right I am.

We still have hard conversations in our marriage and when we are hurt or upset, we discuss those things together. The difference now is our shift in focus from, "I have needs that must be met during this conversation" to, "How can I reestablish and strengthen our heart connection during this conversation?"

One of the ways we practically keep our heart connection strong is to take our issues to God before we attempt to connect with each other. When forgiveness is needed I will intentionally have some time alone to forgive Pieter before I attempt to talk with him. I will sit alone with the Holy Spirit and invite Him to search my heart. The Holy Spirit is so loving and kind and always calls me to a higher way of thinking. Godly sorrow leads to repentance. Repentance means to change the way we think and an invitation to see things from a higher perspective. When I connect with the Holy Spirit, I am asking to see the situation from His perspective. I then forgive Pieter (or myself, if necessary) and repent for any wrongdoing. In God's kindness, He will allow us to feel the pain and conviction, so that we can grow and learn from our experiences. He is a loving Father who corrects us and realigns our thinking with gentleness. We know we are growing spiritually when we start assuming the best in people. Whenever Pieter or anyone else hurts me now, I assume immediately that was not his intention. Whereas before I would think things like, "How could they say that? They obviously don't care about me." Our call as believers is to forgive and also to bless those who have persecuted us or wrongly accused us. Forgiveness aligns our hearts to see things from the Father's perspective. "When someone curses you, bless that person in return. When you are mistreated and harassed by others, accept it as your mission to pray for them." Luke 6:28 TPT

Our mission as believers should be to love others unconditionally. One of the ways we can do this is to walk in forgiveness. The prayer below is a tool you can use for the rest of your life to release forgiveness to others.

Ask Jesus, "Is there anyone I need to forgive today?"

Steps of Forgiveness

1. Repent for holding onto the offense and holding onto any bitterness (Lay down our right to be right and hold on to the pain)
2. Release the person to Jesus
3. Find the lie and/or vow associated with the pain
4. Renounce the lie and the vow
5. Ask Jesus for His Truth (truth will always align with scripture)
6. Ask Jesus to see the heart of the person who hurt you and bless the person who hurt you.

Make a list of who you need to forgive today. The list might be long, and that's ok. Start with family and move on to friends, and people from the past. Then make a list of all the things that you need to forgive yourself for. Lastly, make a list of all the things you need to forgive God for.

_____
_____
_____
_____
_____
_____

Forgiveness Prayer

Lord Jesus, I acknowledge my need for your forgiveness. I believe You are willing to forgive me because of what Jesus paid for when He died on the Cross. But I also acknowledge that I need to forgive others, myself, and even you because of the bitterness I have allowed to remain in my heart. Your word says to aside all bitterness, wrath, anger, clamor, and evil speaking and forgive one another as you have forgiven us in Christ. I know in my heart you are a God of grace. Therefore, please transform my heart and renew my mind by removing any root of bitterness spouting within me because I want a clean and pure heart filled with love, not trouble or poison.

Jesus, I chose to forgive_____ (Name of person, myself or God) for _____. When this happened, I was caused to feel _____ (use the Emotional Pain Words). Just as Jesus took all the pain and consequences of my sin to the cross, I now choose to do the same. So by my own choice, I take the pain and consequences that _____ has caused me to feel to the cross without blame. I relinquish my right to hold onto that pain and nail it to the cross just as you did for me.

Jesus, will you please forgive me for holding onto this right to judge? Somewhere I partnered with a lie that caused me to believe I was entitled to be in control and hold on to this bitterness. I was wrong. Jesus, please take back the ground I gave to the enemy through my agreement with the lies and vows I partnered with. I yield the position of my heart to your control.

Encounter

Jesus, when _____happened, I was _____ (describe how you remember feeling in the moment). My heart is fully surrendered and humble before you know. I need you.

You are a God of comfort, and when _____ (the event or circumstance that caused the pain) happened, I didn't feel comfort. Please, Jesus, show me somehow that in that dark moment, I was not alone. I know you were with me. My heart needs to see you. Where were you?

Jesus, will you please tell me what the lies were that I believed because of what happened? (Write each lie down).

Thank you, Jesus, for helping me reveal the lies I partnered with. I don't want to believe these lies anymore. I want to know in my heart and believe in my mind what the truth is. I want to hear what your truth about me is. Will you please tell me the truth about myself?(Write each truth down- they should never contradict scripture)

Jesus, I am so grateful for what you are doing. Thank you for your grace and love. In your name, Jesus Christ, and by your blood I stand in the courts of Heaven before you as your child and renounce the enemy's accusations and lies I believed _____ (state all the lies).

I now declare to believe the truth of what you say about me

_____ (state all the truths). By your blood, I command the ground of my soul that I surrendered to the enemy to at once be returned to my Lord and Savior, Jesus Christ.

Jesus, I know that you guide me into all the truth. Your word is the lamp to my feet and the light to my path. If I created a vow from the lies I believed that created me to be driven by the enemy and prevented me from following you, I want to know what that vow was so I can break that vow. Jesus, was there a vow I accepted in my heart due to believing a lie about myself? What is that vow?_____.

Jesus, Thank you for shepherding me. You are a good Shepherd who laid down your life for me. I know your voice and longer want to be astray believing the lies the enemy has accused me of. You are the overseer of my soul. Your blood is the eternal covenant. In your name, Jesus Christ, and by your blood I stand in the courts of Heaven before you as your child and break the vow I agreed and entered into with the enemy which stated _____ (state all the vows). I renounce this agreement I made and all the effects it has had on my life. Please deliver me from the drivenness and empowerment I surrendered to the enemy through my agreement. I declare who I am in Christ and exercise the authority You have given me to tread on serpents and scorpions and over all the power of the enemy. I command any influence that the enemy had in my agreement be immediately removed and thrown in the pit of hell.

I no longer am filled with anxiety, fear, or trouble. I receive Your peace. I give You the thanks that Your peace rules in my heart now. You are a God of hope who fills me with joy and peace in believing who You are in me and who I am in You. The power of Your Spirit, which is also in me, abounds in hope. Jesus, I now ask that you fill every part of me with your peace, hope, and joy through this humble surrender to you.

EMOTIONAL PAIN WORDS LIST

Abandoned	Dirty	Invalidated	Stepped on
Accused	Disappointed	Invisible	Shattered
Afraid	Discarded	Isolated	Smothered
All my fault	Discouraged	Knocked down	Stressed
Alone	Disgraced	Judged	Stupid
Always wrong	Dishonored	Left out	Suicidal
Angry	Disregarded	Lied to	Taken advantage of
Annihilated	Disrespected	Lonely	Terrified
Anxious	Dominated	Lost	Threatened
Apathetic	Embarrassed	Made fun of	Torn apart
Ashamed	Empty	Manipulated	Trapped
Awkward	Excluded	Mistreated	Trashed
Bad	Exhausted	Misunderstood	Tripped
Belittled	Exploited	Mocked	Ugly
Betrayed	Exposed	Neglected	Unable to speak
Bewildered	Failure	No good	Unaccepted
Bitter	Fearful	No way out	Undesirable
Blamed	Foolish	Not affirmed	Unfairly judged
Can't measure up	Forsaken	Not cared for	Unfairly treated
Can't trust anyone	Friendless	Not cherished	Unimportant
Cheap	Frightened	Not chosen	Unloved
Cheated	Frustrated	Not heard	Unlovable
Condemned	Good for nothing	Not listen to	Unnecessary
Confused	Guilty	Not needed	Unnoticed
Conspired against	Hated	Not valued	Unprotected
Controlled	Hate myself	Opinions not valued	Unsafe
Crushed	Helpless	Overwhelmed	Unwanted
Cut off	Hopeless	Paralyzed	Useless
Deceived	Humiliated	Powerless	Violated
Defeated	Hurt	Pressured	Vulnerable
Defenseless	Hysterical	Pressured to perform	Walked on
Defrauded	Ignored	Publicly shamed	Wasted
Degraded	Inadequate	Put down rejected	Weak
Depressed	Incompetent	Repulsed	Worthless
Deprived	Inferior	Resentful	Wounded
Deserted	Ignored	Revenge	

Chapter 8

Overcoming Pride - by Pieter Lagaay

"God opposes the proud, but gives grace to the humble."

James 4:6

When Pride is How We Receive Love

I grew up in a home that fostered pride in achievements. It wasn't something that was explicitly expressed. It was more implied and inferred. As a young child I would feel loved and seen when my family would express to me that they were proud of me which usually came on the heels of something I achieved. Let me be clear that I love my family so much, and as a child I wanted nothing more than for them to be proud of me. I still do. But, as a child I believed my family would only be proud of me based on the condition of what I achieved.

My family truly is amazing. Sometimes people hear about my childhood growing up with a mom who was an alcoholic and a father who traveled two weeks out of each month, and wonder how I could say that my family was amazing. I can say it because it is just how my heart feels and what I believe. I know that a lot of people can relate to this statement.

With this being said I will say that my family was not outwardly expressive with love. We didn't say "I love you" to each other. We didn't hug. Instead the love for each other was understood. I hear this a lot from people we minister to when I ask them what their family dynamics were like as a child.

The responses I hear are "I knew my dad or mom loved me, but no we never said I love you or hugged or anything like that." This response is so common and also very representative of how I grew up.

The reason I bring up the lack of outward expression of love in my story while writing a chapter about pride is because until I was healed and delivered I never realized that I associated someone being proud of me as them loving me. Or to take it step further that in order for someone to love then also had to be proud of me. I developed a mindset that love was earned and based on conditional achievements instead of who I was as a person.

So as a child while growing up in a home that didn't say "I love you" but did say "good job", I started to believe that "good job" meant "I love you." I know it might sound a little crazy, but as a child, I was starving for love. Especially when my parents fought because when I heard them screaming at each other I knew there was no love and I wanted it so badly.

Can't Take Pride With You On The Hope Journey

All humans long for connection. We are genetically created to require it. It's what we believe about our relationship with others that reveals the health of our hearts. As I got older, I had no idea how badly I longed for connection and love. My need for the approval of others influenced my mindset and desire for authentic love and relationships. I did many immoral things to feel what my heart desperately needed. I thought I would feel love through viewing porn and sexual encounters, because it made me feel desired. The deception is that love is measured in quality while lust is measured in quantity. I wanted quantity because I didn't know how to experience quality love. The more "good jobs" I got the better I felt about myself. The more sexual attention I got, the more I thought I was worth being desired and wanted.

Over the years I developed a mindset believing I could control how much love I could get through sexual attention to feel loved. The question most people ask when they hear stories like mine about disastrous immorality is "how could this happen? Why didn't you just say no?" I wrestled with those questions for a long time, both before and after I got saved. These questions often start to make me feel shameful and guilty about what I did. For a long time I believed that repeating these questions in my head was actually preventing me from backsliding. I had a "don't ever forget what you did so you never do it again" voice in my head.

Then one day I had a little discussion with God about this.

I was driving to work and asking God, why do I have to keep being reminded of what I did in the past to prevent what I might do in the future. God's answer was very short, "Pieter, who told you that?" So I asked God why I felt so compelled to remind myself of my sinful past. God explained that by looking in the past I was trying to justify my actions. The motivation of trying to justify my past was rooted in pride. God then told me that it was my pride in trying to justify my past that was preventing me from fully being hopeful for my future. The stronghold was that I could not have hope for my future until I would be able to reconcile my past. I had to let go of the pride of being able to explain why I did what I did. I had to let go of all the needing all the answers and just trust and have faith that walking with Jesus would be enough. For a guy who has lived most of his life always needing facts and answers to prove what was real this was a big ask for me. For God it was simple, Pieter how much will you surrender?

The Mirror and Window

My motivation for love was rooted in pride rather than connection. The root of my inability to feel loved by others and myself had developed as a child. I had learned that by getting others to recognize and affirm what I had accomplished I would feel loved. But this was all about me feeling loved. It had nothing to do with connection. The stronghold in my life before I was healed and delivered was that love was a matter of performance. The better I performed or could control something the more love I could get. The problem with this is pride like a mirror. All you see is yourself. Love is a window because you get to see the other person. You can open the window. You can reach through the open window. The window allows a connection. A mirror just redirects your vision back onto yourself.

The fundamental premise of pride is that it directs attention to yourself. Pride has a short fuse and is very quickly threatened. When demonic pride is triggered, impatience and an outward expression of frustration toward others often ensue. The purpose of pride is to direct a focus on yourself. This may be motivated by the insecurity of self-worth, fear of being ignored, unseen, unheard, or another lie stemming from a root wound. Whatever the root of pride is, it builds walls around our hearts.

"Everyone with a proud heart is detestable to the Lord..." Proverbs 16:5 NKJV

The walls of pride prevent others from seeing our hearts and lull us from seeing or feeling the pain in our hearts. Based on the lie that love is conditional, pride is the enemy's tactic to deceive us into believing that pride is necessary to earn or deserve love. If we struggle with pride and performance, the enemy could deceive us of our true identity in who God has created us to be. The sin the enemy is trying to fill our hearts with is often a direct attack on our identity and is the opposite of who God has created us to be. Pride can be a demonic attack on our ability to receive and give unconditional love. If the lie is 'I am filled with pride, and love is conditional,' then the truth of who God says we are is that God created us to be a beacon of hope to demonstrate the unconditional nature of His love!

Inflammatory Pride

Demonic pride can come in two forms. One is a type of pride that inflates, and the other defames (portrays a poor image). Let's first look at inflammatory pride. This type of pride is a "Hey, look at how great I am" type. It is often motivated by seeking the approval of others. I identified with inflammatory pride in the past. Inflammatory pride has a condition attached to it. Do this and receive that. It's not free because you have to do something. Much of inflammatory pride stems from a belief system that in order to achieve anything it must be done in your own strength. As a result, performance and work ethic becomes tainted by this drivenness of the enemy. This demonic drive is based on self hate and lies. Sanctified perseverance is led by God's truth and love for you.

During my healing and deliverance, I received the revelation of what motivated me to obsessively value the approval of others by understanding my story like how God perceived it. In that moment I experienced His unconditional love by walking up the steps of surrender to the door of the Father's heart. The revelation during this encounter empowered my brain to recognize the lie I believed because of what my heart felt. This beautiful encounter with Father God and moment of deliverance from the stronghold of pride was powerful, but it was His mercy to reveal this to me that immediately caused me to repent for how I loved my kids.

I know my kids want to make me happy. They are amazing and I love them so much. I am very proud of them. I believe that they know that if they do something I don't like, it doesn't change how much I love them. Regardless of what they say and do, I love them because they are my kids. The important part about all this is that my kids feel loved no matter what and without conditions. It wasn't always like that.

I used to get very frustrated and impatient with them. I am sure they knew I loved them, but they didn't feel very loved by me in those moments.

For many years, I attached many conditions to my approval for them. It wasn't until this moment of revelation when I was delivered of pride that I was overcome with a powerful conviction to heal the relationship with my kids.

Defamatory Pride

The other form of pride creates a victim mentality. This is defamatory because it causes us to be viewed as weak and less than others. Defamatory pride still directs attention to ourselves for the same reason as inflammatory pride, but in a different manner. Defamatory pride directs attention toward a person as self-pity. It aims to seek attention through pity from others. It manipulates others into giving us attention through guilt and shame. Defamatory pride portrays an image of identity that is weak, poor, and hurt to seek attention. In essence, it creates a victim mindset in us. It might seem like this is not pride because the common perception of pride is that it always puffs up. But when the outward expression of actions are motivated to gain attention unto ourselves, it is a form of pride.

Position vs. Posture

Identifying unhealthy pride, whether inflammatory or defamatory, depends on the position of our heart. To be clear, the position of our heart is different from the posture of our heart. Let me explain what I mean by this.

Posture is how we intentionally or even habitually hold our position. Our hearts can be positioned in any way. That's part of the free will God empowered us with. It becomes a posture when we intentionally or habitually maintain a certain position. The motivation or reason for holding that particular posture is rooted in a truth or lie we believe, a stronghold. Why we posture our hearts in a certain way is usually because we want to hide or prevent something about ourselves from being exposed. When we posture our heart to hide from circumstances or people it is usually done in reaction to emotions which stir up pain, fear, self-condemnation, or any other negative emotions. One of those postures can be pride.

The posture of pride is something we choose to do. We may not fully recognize it at the moment because our posture will feel like we are in a very natural position, but our bodies are meant to move, not be held in a stagnant fixed position. In medicine, there is a saying, "Motion is the key to life." In scripture, this motion is equated to hope. When we lose hope, we lose life. The ability to move is paramount because it enables us to turn away from that unhealthy posture and be free to position ourselves before the truth of what God says about us. Repentance is the catalyst used to get our hearts out of a posture of pride and into a position of humility. It is the heart of the Father and His grace that enable us to be confident in our vulnerability and celebrate the freedom from pride that is solely obtained by the power of the blood of Jesus. Here is an example in my life about how repentance broke the posture of pride in my life to a position of humility.

Repositioning Through Repentance

I had just finished my medical residency and foot and ankle trauma fellowship. I felt like I had conquered the world. I was hired by a hospital and asked to be a research director. I was invited to speak at numerous conferences and teach students and residents. Professionally, I was so incredibly blessed. But what was the position of my heart? I mentioned before that I was raised in a family that affirmed me mainly through my achievements. So, I learned to seek out affirmation through my accomplishments. The affirmation I sought was love, but since I didn't understand what healthy love looked or felt like, I would seek affirmation in the form of pride by professional accomplishment, sexual attention, and material gain. My heart wanted love, and deep down, I was hurting because I didn't know how to connect in love or receive love. I wanted a window but just had a mirror.

I didn't have the language to articulate this either because I was unaware. When I felt like I was not being affirmed, I would feel pain. I had no grid for the pain, or why it was there, so I would try harder. I felt better when I got the affirmation I sought, but only briefly. So I decided that to prevent this very uncomfortable feeling for which I had no language for, I would posture my heart in a certain way to feel better. I intentionally held a position of my heart to hide from having to expose how I was feeling. This was my heart posture, and it was demonic pride.

Free Will

Recognizing our heart posture is vital because it tells us what to repent from and what to repent to. I didn't realize the posture of my own heart was pride until after I went through inner healing and deliverance. Just like how I had chosen to hold a position and form a posture of pride, I also had to be willing to turn towards a truth I didn't know yet in faith. That is very scary and gives the word surrender real context. As I turned away from holding onto control to prevent feeling the uncomfortableness and uncertainties of what might happen, the power of God's love wrecked me in a way that remains vivid even in my sleep. Remember when I said that the catalyst to move from a posture of pride to a position of humility and vulnerability is repentance? Well, the catalyst of repentance can't drive the reaction to turn without the element of free will to surrender. Just like how we have free will to hold a position and go into a demonic posture, we have free will to surrender to Jesus to be healed and delivered from this posture. For me, that free will to surrender was anchored in hope. I didn't have a lot. I had lost all my professional accomplishments and felt like a total failure as a man, husband, father, and doctor. The little hope I had was mostly from others. I used their hope to surrender and repent. This meant giving up my control to hold this posture so God could position me where I needed to be.

Have you ever seen a kid holding onto something so tight and not knowing how to let go to receive help? I think of a child learning to hold a baseball bat. They grip the bat incorrectly and hold on so tight. But they won't let go, so they can be shown how to hold the bat correctly. First, you have to peel their little fingers off the bat and remold them. Then, you can position the bat correctly by bending their elbows and wrists. Now, when the kid swings, the likelihood of success in hitting the ball is much greater. Moving from a posture of pride to a position of humility is like that. We hold onto that posture of pride so tightly, and we sometimes don't know how to let go. For me, God had to peel my grip from holding onto pride so that I could realize I could let go! But things are much easier if you just voluntarily let go of the bat, but that's a story for another day.

"Humble yourselves before the Lord, and he will exalt you." James 4:10 ESV

So, what am I saying about pride? I am saying that it is in God's goodness we find hope. If we can't find it there, use the hope other people have for you. This hope, along with the surrender, is the first step in repenting our posture of pride. Once we surrender our control of what we think we have a right to believe in then God can loosen our grip on the posture of pride. The rest is easy because that moment of surrender creates tremendous vulnerability and builds our faith. In that moment, we pray with repentance and faith that God is good so that we can receive His grace and unconditional love through a tangible encounter that transforms our hearts and renews our minds. Our heart then becomes positioned with His, and the manifestation is peace which surpasses all understanding. .

Prayer for Freedom from Pride

Lord Jesus, I confess that I have sinned against you through my prideful behavior exhibited by _____ (say out loud areas of pride the Holy Spirit reveals to you). I renounce this prideful behavior along with any and all legal agreements that were made by allowing my heart to be motivated with pride. Jesus, please forgive me for opening the door of my soul to pride through my behaviors and thoughts. I yield any part of my soul that I have surrendered to the enemy through my prideful thoughts and behaviors to your control. You are my Lord and savior and I relinquish any right that I might have believed to justify my pride to you. I ask that you please break any and all bondage in my life and my children and generations to follow that have resulted from my prideful behavior and thoughts. Jesus please fill all the vacated parts of my soul that were once occupied by demonic strongholds with your Holy Spirit and Shalom Peace. Thank you Lord Jesus for what you have done both on the Cross and right now. The power of your blood has authority over all and I celebrate that now with the freedom you have given me. Jesus please give me the strength, courage and wisdom to not partner with prideful behavior or thoughts thereby keeping my soul pure made in your image.

Chapter 9

Redeeming Purity and Sex in Marriage - by Pieter Lagaay

"For of this you can be sure: No immoral, impure or greedy person—such a person is an idolater—has any inheritance in the kingdom of Christ and of God."

Ephesians 5:5 NIV

This chapter is generally not met with great excitement and anticipation. At least, that is how I felt when I went through my inner healing and deliverance. The biggest reason was because I knew the road to redeeming my purity had to go through facing my moral failure and there was a lot of guilt and shame in that. I was terrified to expose all the moral failures in my life because the shame and guilt told me it was unforgivable. I believed my sin was better left hidden because what I had done could not be forgiven. But let me tell you before we start, I am not a bad person, and neither are you. You are a child of God and are made in His image. You are worthy of being forgiven and can forgive others that have hurt you. A father doesn't want his child to live in guilt and shame, and Father God doesn't want you to either! Therefore, not only can you be redeemed and restored, but you will be redeemed and restored! This chapter is dear to my heart because moral failure nearly killed me and my marriage. Jesus healed my heart of shame and guilt, but most importantly, He healed the hurt in my heart that drove me to seek out sexual sin. I can testify today that I am no longer bound to immorality because Jesus showed up for me in my most vulnerable state, and He will for you too. Jesus always shows up!

"He heals the broken-hearted and binds up their wounds." Psalm 147:3 NKJV

Certain moral failures may resonate and be familiar to many of us, but the pain in the heart that drives one person's moral failure is usually very unique. This is why I believe healing the wounds of our heart that tempt and cause us to sin in moral failure truly need an encounter with Jesus to be free from bondage. I have had a few encounters centered around my moral failure, but the most significant was in a dream when I saw the face of God. When I have led other men through their own moral failures, God always reveals a truth about themselves that somehow in their lives was forgotten.

"Then you will know the truth and the truth will set you free." John 8:32 NIV

Recently I heard someone at my men's group say that our sin is not the problem. Instead, it is the solution to the pain we are feeling and the lies we believe. This can be a hard statement to agree with because a common stronghold is that by not focusing on the sin, we are hiding or failing to be responsible for our actions. That is not true. We are responsible for what we sow, which is probably why you are reading this. "You reap what you sow…" Galatians 6:7 (paraphrased). When I decided to go through inner healing and deliverance, I wanted freedom now. For many years of my life, I believed that I had a sin problem. It wasn't until after inner healing and deliverance that I realized that the genesis of my sin was in a perverted identity. What I believed about my identity was the problem because it was rooted in lies and demonic vows.

"Don't you know that when you allow even a little lie into your heart, it can permeate your entire belief system?" Galatians 5:9 TPT

Authentic Connection

Let me try to frame this in a general way. We are created to be in connection. We were not created to be alone. Some people enjoy alone time more than others, but as humans, we are not genetically engineered to be isolated for extended periods. It is physiologically and psychologically unhealthy for us. With that being understood, as children, we crave and need connection. This is demonstrated by a study I once saw. It is a video of a baby who is about one year old. She is sitting in a highchair and playing with a woman. This woman is fully engaged with this baby. The baby is excited about playing with this woman and having a connection. Then on a command from the study personnel, the woman stops playing with the baby and turns her back to the baby. The baby continues to play for a few seconds. Then the baby realizes the connection is absent and tries to get the woman's attention. As a minute passes, the baby becomes frantic, crying and screaming. After only a couple of minutes, the woman is instructed to turn back and reconnect with the baby. The baby continues to scream and cry. It takes the woman about 5 minutes to calm the baby down, and the baby does not re-engage in playing and having the original level of connection.

So why do I bring this up? Because we need connection. Once a connection is established, we need to maintain it. But we also need to know how to create it. We need to know how to deal with the pain of a lost connection. In many of the people that Melinda and I have counseled, I have seen connections broken and never established as a child. If we are not taught how to create, maintain and steward connections with others, then we seek out a connection in unhealthy ways that may involve moral failure.

Identifying the Root

I grew up in a home where my dad traveled a lot. He also came from a generation that believed it was best to not be emotional because it was weak and unstable. My mom was an alcoholic and unavailable because she was sleeping a lot. So I didn't have a lot of connection as a child with the people with whom children are supposed to have the most connection. If we are created for connection and don't feel connected with the people who brought us into this world, then it's hard to continue and build a connection with others. I am not trying to place blame. There is no healing in fault. I am trying to establish an understanding of the root of my pain.

I had no idea the root of my sinful behavior, in the context of moral failure, was in my need for connection and a fear of failure and rejection.

"Make sure that no one falls short of the grace of God and that no root of bitterness springs up, causing trouble and defiling many." Hebrews 12:15.

I thought I had a discipline problem. But when I invited Jesus into my heart and asked him to show me how I learned about connection and was introduced to the many lies I believed about myself growing up. I believed I could only achieve connection through my accomplishments, achievements and that a physical connection was the same as a heart connection. Lastly, I thought I wasn't worthy of connection because I didn't deserve it. This caused me to fear rejection, so I hid everything in my life that might cause me to feel rejected.

When I needed connection, I didn't know how to get it in a healthy manner, so I would do what felt good in the flesh. You see, a connection is just as much spiritual as it is physical. Let me explain it like this. I can experience God physically by witnessing miracles through prayer and experiencing blessings.

Still, suppose I don't have a spiritual or relational connection, a real heart-to-heart with God that I can explain because it is hidden deep in me. In that case, it is hard for me to experience connection as it is intended to be experienced. The same can be said with my wife. If I get to be alone with my wife for the entire weekend or week, I get lots of physical time because I can see and hug her the whole time. But if I don't get to connect with her on a heart-to-heart level, then I still don't have that real connection.

You Are Not a Failure, You Are Righteous

I have heard so many people, whether single or married, say something is missing in life. Many times it is a connection. Without connection, we pick up sinful behavior to comfort our pain. Moral failure is a failure, but it's not unredeemable. It is momentary, not evolutionary; meaning a moral failure does mean I have become a failure. God uses all things for His good. I have seen this in my life personally and in many others who I have counseled. It starts with a surrender and exercising our free will to bring out what the enemy wants you to believe needs to stay hidden.

Moral failure is just that and only that. It's not your identity, nor who you are meant to be. The moment you speak it out with your heart positioned before God and ask for his forgiveness, you will already experience a tremendous breakthrough. Don't hold anything back. Be brave and know that love conquers all and that the perfect love of the Father casts out all fear (1 John 4:18). It is scary to speak out our deepest secrets, but when this is received with love, a true transformation of the heart and renewing of the mind happens. I have experienced it personally and seen it time and time again. Jesus always shows up!

Prayer for Freedom from Sexual Sin

Lord Jesus, I confess that I have sinned against you through my moral failure exhibited by _____ (ask the Holy Spirit to highlight specific areas of sin that need to be renounced). I renounce my sexual sin along with any and all legal agreements that were made by allowing my sinful behavior to serve as a coping mechanism for the wounds in my heart. I repent for desiring someone else's love more than yours. Jesus, please forgive me for opening the door of my soul to being immoral through my actions and thoughts. I yield any part of my soul that I have surrendered to the enemy through my immoral actions and behavior to your control.

In Jesus' name I take authority over all spirits of sexual sin, and I break their hold over my life. You are my Lord and savior and I relinquish any and all desire of control to prevent having to face the pain in my heart and also give you any and all guilt and shame that I have claimed because I believed the lie that I wasn't good enough for you. You created me and love me just like the prodigal son or daughter. You are my truth and you just want my surrendered heart no matter what it looks like.

In Jesus' name I break any and all bondage in my life and my children and generations to follow that have resulted from my sexual sin. Jesus please fill all the vacated parts of my soul that were once occupied by demonic strongholds with your Holy Spirit and Shalom Peace. Thank you Lord Jesus for what you have done both on the Cross and right now. The power of your blood has authority over all and I celebrate that now with the freedom you have given me. Jesus please give me the strength, courage and wisdom to not partner with immorality thereby keeping my soul pure made in your image.

Breaking Soul-tie Prayer (Soul ties can be emotional or sexual)

Lord Jesus, in your name and by the power of your blood, please separate my body, soul, and spirit, from the body, soul, and spirit of_____. In the name and by the blood of the Lord Jesus Christ, I command all evil spirits and all of their networks that transferred to me to be pulled out by the roots, to look at the blood of Jesus, and to get out of me and go where the Lord Jesus Christ sends you, forever. Lord Jesus, please fill each empty space of my body, soul and spirit with your Holy Spirit and. your supernatural peace.

Chapter 10

Breaking Free from Witchcraft and the Occult

"The Holy Spirit has explicitly revealed: As the end of this age, many will depart from the truth faith one after another, devouring themselves to spirits or deception and following demon-inspired revelations and theories."

1 Timothy 4:1 TPT

Years ago we received a call from a friend regarding a ministry school student who needed deliverance. Throughout the interview process we discovered "Hurting Hillary" had been a prostitute for many years. Hurting Hillary would use the money she earned as a prostitute to consult a psychic who would "help" give her direction for her life. Hurting Hillary was also a first generation Christian. First generation Christians are contending for freedom and blessings that have been withheld in a bloodline for generations.

We spent two hours with Hurting Hillary and listened to her story. We uncovered that she had been plagued with nightmares, suicidal thoughts, and anger. Hurting Hillary could not stand long in worship service for long periods of time or demons would start manifesting.

We started the session by praying and inviting the Holy Spirit to give us wisdom and discernment. As soon as we started praying, Hurting Hillary started manifesting demonically. Her hands contorted and her face changed into what looked like an animal. Hurting Hillary was typically very soft-spoken and was suddenly barking at us, growling at us, and telling us to shut up. We knew we were no longer talking to Hurting Hillary, but to the demons that were tormenting her. We commanded the demons to speak only when instructed and we commanded them to tell us the truth. We found out Hurting Hillary had been a prostitute for many years and used the money from prostitution to consult the psychic. The doors Hurting Hillary had opened into the demonic realm had given the demons permission to be present in her life.

"Now the works of the flesh are evident, which are: adultery, fornication, uncleanness, lewdness, idolatry, sorcery, hatred, contentions, jealousies, outbursts of wrath, selfish ambitions, dissensions, heresies," Galatians 5:19-20 NKJV

What Happens When People Consult Psychics?

Psychics claim to foresee the future, but they actually access information about a person's past and current circumstances through divination - communicating with demons. By revealing such personal details, they gain people's trust to then make prophecies and encourage further consultations to "avoid misfortune." Yet their supernatural "wisdom" comes from demons, not dead relatives. Psychics use divination to lure people into believing their destiny is predestined and only by consulting the psychic can it be controlled. But their prophecies are deceptive. The truth is, psychics commune with demonic spirits, not deceased loved ones. Those who have sought psychics or engaged in witchcraft should renounce these acts and seek deliverance. For the future lies not in psychic predictions, but in God's hands.

During her deliverance session, the normally soft-spoken Hurting Hillary began manifesting demonic spirits through spitting, barking, and hissing. We discerned the demons were present due to sexual sin and had her repent. Yet they still refused to leave. We asked under the anointing and blood of Jesus, "Do you have any other legal right to be in Hillary's life?"

Forced to tell the truth, the demons revealed her unforgiveness toward her father. Though she had repented of sexual sin, bitterness kept her bound. Only by addressing the unresolved anger against her father could Hurting Hillary's deliverance be completed. Forgiveness would break the legal grounds holding her captive.

When we asked Hurting Hillary if she needed to forgive her father, she exclaimed, "Yes! I hate him!" We explained that her unforgiveness was keeping her bound. Forgiveness did not mean allowing her father back into her life or removing necessary boundaries, we clarified. Rather, it meant releasing her hatred and bitterness toward him. The demons tormenting her had legal rights because of her unforgiveness. If she was willing to relinquish her resentment and leave judgment of her father to Jesus, she could be freed from their hold. With this understanding, Hurting Hillary saw that forgiving her father was the key to breaking free from the spiritual bondage she had been suffering under.

"Beloved, do not avenge yourselves, but rather give place to wrath; for it is written, "Vengeance is Mine, I will repay," says the Lord." Romans 12:19 NKJV

Harboring unforgiveness towards our parents violates one of God's spiritual laws to respect and honor our parents.

"Honor your father and mother," which is the first commandment with promise: that it may be well with you and you may live long on the earth." Ephesians 6:2-3 NKJV

Though initially resistant, Hurting Hillary became willing to forgive her father for the trauma he had caused. We walked her through a prayer releasing him from her judgment.

In doing so, many lies and vows emerged that Hurting Hillary had embraced about herself and God stemming from her father's abuse.

Hurting Hillary renounced each one and welcomed the Holy Spirit's truth - that she was a precious, beloved child of God.

With forgiveness and truth lifting legal grounds, the tormenting demons had to flee. Hurting Hillary was finally delivered from their affliction. We then addressed her past sin of consulting a psychic. This had opened a doorway to the demonic that Hurting Hillary witchcraft repentance now closed. As she renounced that involvement, those spirits too were forced to leave, shrieking as deliverance was completed. Forgiveness and repentance brought long-awaited freedom. Hurting Hillary had unlocked the chains of the past through God's grace.

"Many evil spirits were cast out, screaming as they left their victims. And many who had been paralyzed or lame were healed. So there was great joy in that city." Acts of the Apostles 8:7-8 NLT

Nothing is too hard for the power and blood of Jesus, but oftentimes it is ignorance that leads people to remain in bondage. Jesus died so we could be free, but we must understand how the spirit realm works. Our job is to partner with God by repenting, renouncing for the sins we have committed and the sins of our ancestors. Yes, the blood of Jesus paid for our freedom, but we are often unaware that we need to apply the blood of Jesus to each circumstance (past, present and future) in our lives. It is the blood of Jesus, the power of the resurrection, and the anointing of the Holy Spirit that sets us free.

"But He was wounded for our transgressions, He was bruised for our iniquities; The chastisement for our peace was upon Him, And by His stripes we are healed. All we like sheep have gone astray; We have turned, every one, to his own way; And the Lord has laid on Him the iniquity of us all." Isaiah 53:5-6 NKJV

Our generation is seeking something supernatural because we were created in the image of God and we are supernatural beings. The Bible says we were created before the foundations of the world. This includes believers and unbelievers. Part of the problem is Christians have become completely unaware of the spirit realm. "Set your mind on things above, not on things on the earth." (Colossians 3:2).

The devil simply doesn't care if you go to church, tithe, sing, go to a potluck, or make new friends. As long as you are not moving in power, casting out demons, or stepping into higher levels of freedom and authority, you are not a threat to the devil and his kingdom. Lukewarm Christians who are not moving in power are the devil's love language. They are simply not a threat to him.

Witchcraft and the occult are very much alive and happening today throughout the United States and throughout the world. We have seen the devastating effects of witchcraft on families and individuals. People who need deliverance from witchcraft tend to have the most physical manifestations. We have seen people slithering on the floor in the form of a snake and moving their bodies in ways that are not physically possible in the natural realm without breaking a bone. We have had a woman try to bite us (in an extreme case) and try to tell us to shut up (among many other things).

We have helped victims of SRA (Satanic Ritual Abuse) where blood pacts have been made and some of them were dedicated to Satan. We have seen faces contort and bodies bend in ways not humanly possible as demons manifest. We have seen snakes leave bodies and people hiss and growl at us like wild animals. We have seen people throw up as demons are leaving their bodies. We have ministered to individuals that participated in Freemason and were later healed physically after repenting for their involvement.

Each time we minister deliverance to someone we see something new. That is simply because each individual is unique and has a unique background. Many times we will learn on the spot, but one thing never changes. The Holy Spirit is always our guide, and we always minister in LOVE. We simply could not do it without the precious and powerful person of the Holy Spirit.

Individuals Needing Deliverance from Witchcraft Should Always Be Ministered To In Love.

We have seen horrible deliverances that involved yelling loudly at the person and the demons, but demons simply do not respond to yelling. Demons respond to authority and they know who has it and who does not. It is important to know you can ask which demon is present and they must respond. However, if you are dealing with someone who has dabbled in divination you will almost always find a python spirit. Divination is taken from a greek word "puton" which means "python." Snakes are often found in the soul or body and can affect people physically.

Christians cannot be possessed, but there are different levels of oppression that can lead to severe manifestations in the natural realm. Generally, the level the ancestors participated in the occult affects the severity of the deliverance.

"Do not turn to mediums or seek out spiritists, for you will be defiled by them. I am the LORD your God." Leviticus 19:31 NKJV

We have ministered deliverance to individuals from various countries. Each country has its own set of demonic powers and false gods. People with ancestors who have a Hindu background for example could need deliverance for the worship of false gods their ancestors practiced. People from Brazil have a whole different set of witchcraft such as Macumba. People from Germany many times have ancestors who were Nazis. We have casted out demons of supremacy and Nazi demons. The list of what we have encountered is long.

The individuals we have mentioned in the above stories are not at fault. They have come under the control of demonic forces that are trying to destroy them and their families. Many of the individuals we have helped have not participated in witchcraft, but their mother, father or grandparents, or great-grandparents participated.

"When this became known to the Jews and Greeks living in Ephesus, they were all seized with fear, and the name of the Lord Jesus was held in high honor. Many of those who believed now came and openly confessed what they had done. A number who had practiced sorcery brought their scrolls together and burned them publicly. When they calculated the value of the scrolls, the total came to fifty thousand drachmas. In this way the word of the Lord spread widely and grew in power." Acts 19:17-20 NIV

My experience in the occult was extremely mild compared to many I have ministered to.

When I was a child I went to a sleepover with a group of friends. One of my friends brought a Ouija Board. I had never seen one before, so I was curious. Something in my heart told me that this was not a good idea, but I did not want to be the one that ended the fun, since I was desperate to fit in with this group of girls.

To play the game, we lit some candles, turned off the lights and sat in a circle in a dark room. We started by asking the "magical" board a question. We were trying to communicate with one of the girl's dead relatives. Suddenly, the game piece on the center of the board began to move.

Everyone looked around to see who was doing it. We all giggled nervously, as we secretly wondered who was moving the game piece. I was scared, so I was really hoping one of my friends would confess.

The piece moved from letter to letter as we asked "yes" or "no" questions. We all thought we were communicating with the dead relative, but then someone asked the question, "Is this really Jim?" (The name of the relative was changed for privacy purposes). The board moved to spell, "No." Then suddenly all of the candles in the room blew out! None of the windows were opened and there was no wind in the room. All of the girls screamed (including me)! Thankfully, someone got up and turned the lights back on. To say we were frightened was an understatement!

Since this experience I have learned that games such as the Ouija Board might seem innocent and just "fun and games," but they are actually a portal into the demonic realm.

"The acts of the flesh are obvious: sexual immorality, impurity and debauchery; idolatry and witchcraft; hatred, discord, jealousy, fits of rage, selfish ambition, dissensions, factions." Galatians 5:19-20 NIV

The enemy loves for us to think childhood games are not a big deal, but Satan is the father of lies and masquerades as an angel of light (see John 8:44 and 2 Corinthians 11:14). Satan loves to put a fun or pretty bow on things that are demonic. Think of how sneaky it is to create a game for children that is a direct portal to demons. Children are innocently opening a demonic door and have no idea they just participated in witchcraft.

"But the cowardly, the unbelieving, the vile, the murderers, the sexually immoral, those who practice magic arts, the idolaters and all liars—they will be consigned to the fiery lake of burning sulfur. This is the second death." Revelation 21:8 NIV

"The Holy Spirit has explicitly revealed: As the end of this age, many will depart from the truth faith one after another, devouring themselves to spirits or deception and following demon-inspired revelations and theories." 1 Timothy 4:1 TPT

Breaking Generational Curses

The good news is we have authority over all of the power of the enemy, so we can renounce and repent for anything that we participated in.

Repenting for the sins of your ancestors is called "Identificational Repentance." Examples of Identificational Repentance can be found in Nehemiah 1:6-9, and 1 Corinthians 7:14. Again, nothing can be done without the power of the Holy Spirit. It is the Holy Spirit that anoints believers to set people free. It is because of this wonderful privilege that we are able to set others free in love. Only the blood of Jesus covers our sins and the power of the Holy Spirit that sets us free. What an awesome privilege to see the captives set free!

"The Spirit of the Sovereign Lord is on me, because the Lord has anointed me to proclaim good news to the poor. He has sent me to bind up the brokenhearted, to proclaim freedom for the captives and release from darkness for the prisoners,[a] to proclaim the year of the Lord's favor and the day of vengeance of our God, to comfort all who mourn, and provide for those who grieve in Zion—to bestow on them a crown of beauty instead of ashes, the oil of joy instead of mourning, and a garment of praise instead of a spirit of despair. They will be called oaks of righteousness, a planting of the Lord for the display of his splendor." Isaiah 61:1-3 NIV

Prayer To Break Free from Witchcraft Or Occult

Lord Jesus, I confess that I, and/or my upline, have sinned against you through involvement in. _____

_____

I renounce the occult behavior and activities I, and/or, my upline has participated in. I renounce any and all legal agreements that were made through either my or my uplines engagement in these occult activities. Jesus, please forgive me and/or my upline from opening the door of my soul to the occult through my activities. I yield any part of my soul that I and/or my upline have surrendered to the enemy through my and/or my upline participation in the occult to your control.

Jesus, I ask that you please break any and all bondage in my life and my children and generations to follow that have resulted from my and/or my uplines involvement with the occult. Jesus please fill all the vacated parts of my soul that were once occupied by demonic strongholds with your Holy Spirit and Shalom Peace. Thank you Lord Jesus for what you have done both on the Cross and today. The power of blood has authority over all and I celebrate that now with the freedom you have given me. Jesus please give me the strength, courage and wisdom to not partner with occult activities thereby keeping my soul pure made in your image.

Chapter 11

Freedom from Hypocrisy

Hypocrisy is the "plastic you." A fake version of yourself in order to look good in front of others. With the explosion of the internet and the online world, it's easy to put a fake version of yourself out there for others to see. I know I have done this many times, and have to check myself before I post things on social media. The question I always ask myself is: "Why am I posting this? To look good in front of others or because I think it will help someone?" Hypocrisy is always an issue of the heart.

"But the Lord said to Samuel, "Do not consider his appearance or his height, for I have rejected him. The Lord does not look at the things people look at. People look at the outward appearance, but the Lord looks at the heart." 1 Samuel 16:7 NIV

Biblically, when we are being hypocritical, we are doing things like: telling others to live a godly life, while we live in secret the exact opposite of a godly life. This can include telling others how close we are to God, but rarely praying. Or this can look like telling others what a great marriage we have, but barely put time in to communicate with our spouse. Or this can look like preaching on purity, and meanwhile, you are watching porn at home. Or this can look like you acting kind to your children in front of others at church, and meanwhile, screaming at your kids at home. Jesus pointed out hypocrisy in the religious leaders, and spent a great deal of time teaching on this subject in Matthew 23. Jesus spoke to the crowds and said about the Pharisees (religious leaders):

"So you must be careful to do everything they tell you. But do not do what they do, for they do not practice what they preach." Matthew 23:3 NIV

"Woe to you, scribes and Pharisees, hypocrites! You clean the outside of the cup and dish, but inside they are full of greed and self-indulgence." Matthew 23:25 NIV

Pointing out hypocrisy is not for condemnation, but it is a chance to repent (change the way we think) about the priorities of our heart. We find the root of why we feel the need to put forth a fake version of ourselves. Hypocrisy is always an issue of the heart. Pieter and I had to repent for being hypocrites in many areas of our lives. We repent for being hypocritical towards God and towards others.

Prayer for Freedom from Hypocrisy

Lord Jesus, I confess that I have sinned against you through my hypocritical behavior, thoughts and or beliefs exhibited by _____

_____ (get specific as the Holy Spirit leads you). I renounce my hypocrisy along with any and all legal agreements that were made by allowing my heart to be motivated by fear or man and any other lie that I believed. Jesus, please forgive me for opening the door of my soul to being hypocritical through my behaviors and thoughts. I yield any part of my soul that I have surrendered to the enemy through my hypocritical behavior, thoughts and or beliefs to your control.

You are my Lord and savior and I relinquish any and all desire of control to make myself look better because of lies that I believed. You created me and are always with me. You are my truth and your thoughts of me are all that matter. I ask that you please break any and all bondage in my life and my children and generations to follow that have resulted from my hypocritical behavior, thoughts and or beliefs. Jesus please fill all the vacated parts of my soul that were once occupied by demonic strongholds with your Holy Spirit and Shalom Peace.

Thank you Lord Jesus for what you have done both on the Cross and right now. The power of your blood has authority over all and I celebrate that now with the freedom you have given me. Jesus please give me the strength, courage and wisdom to not partner with hypocrisy thereby keeping my soul pure made in your image.

CHAPTER 12

WORSHIPING IDOLS

"How could you worship two gods at the same time? You will have to hate one and love the other, or be devoted to one and despise the other. You can't worship the true God while enslaved to the god of money."

Matthew 6:24 TPT

Money is not evil in itself, but the love of money, power, and possessions, is evil. This is why Jesus tells us it's easier for a camel to make it through the eye of a needle than get into heaven (paraphrased). This parable in Matthew 19:24 refers to an actual place in Jerusalem. When Jesus was speaking to the disciples about the eye of the needle He may have been referencing a small gate that allows passage into Jerusalem. This small gate is actually named "The Eye of the Needle." When people would travel from afar to enter Jerusalem they loaded their possessions on their camels. A camel loaded with all these possessions was too bulky to fit through the The Eye of the Needle gate. So if someone wanted to enter Jerusalem through this gate, they had to first unload their possessions, then the camel would fit through. So perhaps what Jesus is saying is to unload the possessions of your metaphorical camel so it's easier to enter the Kingdom of God.

God loves to bless us, but does not like when anything replaces our first love for Jesus. An "idol" is not a statue that you put in your home to worship, although it can be that. For most of us today "idols" are anything we put on the metaphorical throne of our lives above a relationship with God. Idols can be the desire for power, money, people, personal, career, possessions or even social media. Idols can be anything that turns our affection away from Jesus. Our heart must value pleasing God and knowing Him above all other things in our life. The most important command is to love God.

"Jesus said to him, '"You shall love the Lord your God with all your heart, with all your soul, and with all your mind.' This is the first and great commandment. And the second is like it: ' You shall love your neighbor as yourself.' On these two commandments hang all the Law and the Prophets." Matthew 22:37-40 NKJV

There is nothing wrong with having possessions or having money. Believers need money to advance the Kingdom of God! I believe God desires to bless believers financially. The real issue is always an issue of the heart.

"For where your treasure is, there your heart will be also." Matthew 6:21 NKJV

Prayer for Freedom from Idols

Lord Jesus, I confess that I have sinned against you through my idolatry exhibited by_____ (get specific as the Holy Spirit leads you). I renounce my idolatry along with any and all legal agreements that were made by allowing my heart to value what the world says is valuable rather than you. Jesus, please forgive me for opening the door of my soul to idolatry through my behaviors and thoughts. I yield any part of my soul that I have surrendered to the enemy through my idolatry to your control. You are my Lord and savior and I relinquish any and all desire for material things, approval from others, and accomplishments demonstrating what I can do in my own strength to you. You created me and you are all I need and want. You are my provider and a God of abundance. I will never lack anything with you. I ask that you please break any and all bondage in my life and my children and generations to follow that have resulted from my idolatry. Jesus please fill all the vacated parts of my soul that were once occupied by demonic strongholds with your Holy Spirit and Shalom Peace. Thank you Lord Jesus for what you have done both on the Cross and right now. The power of your blood has authority over all and I celebrate that now with the freedom you have given me. Jesus please give me the strength, courage and wisdom to not partner with idolatry thereby keeping my soul pure made in your image.

Chapter 13

Freedom from Rebellion

"Rebellion is as sinful as witchcraft and stubbornness as bad as worshiping idols…"

1 Samuel 15:23 NLT

Rebellion is defiance in our hearts towards others or God. When we have a rebellious attitude in our hearts we are not teachable or correctable. We have all been around someone with a stubborn, unteachable attitude, and it is not fun! I have had that sort of attitude myself at times in the past. When I was hurt I would rebel out of the pain I was feeling in my heart. People can also rebel out of pride, or feelings or superiority over those who are in leadership. Rebellion is all about control. When we feel out of control, or we have felt that way in the past, we rebel to gain back the control we feel like we lost. Ultimately, rebellion is defiance in our hearts towards God and God's plan for us.

"Therefore, as the Holy Spirit says, "Today, if you hear His voice, do not harden your hearts as in the rebellion, on the day of testing in the wilderness." Hebrews 3:7-8 NKJV

Control

Control is what Jezabel did when she married King Ahab. Jezabel had all of the prophets killed, and she worshiped the god Baal. Control and rebellion are the source of the "Jezebel spirit." When we want to be in control we can rebel against leadership and authority in our homes, churches, governments, and in our jobs. When we think of the word "rebellion" we can think of Satan who demonstrated what it looks like to rebel against God. Satan was in heaven near God and he still fell and rebelled against God. This was the first recorded act of pride that resulted in rebellion against God.

There are circumstances in which you should not submit to leaders or others. This includes when people are being physically or spiritually abused. We must all act fast to get ourselves out of those situations, and report the event to the authorities. What we are talking about is a general attitude of "you can't tell me what to do" that stems from pride and rebellion. When we have this heart posture of pride, we prevent God from working in our lives, because we are trying to control everything and everyone.

Prayer to break free from Rebellion

Dear Jesus, I humbly confess that I have sinned against You through my rebellious behavior, thoughts, and beliefs, as shown by_____ _____(get specific as the Holy Spirit leads you). Today, I choose to let go of my rebellion and any agreements I made that stemmed from a wounded heart, where I tried to control others and my circumstances out of fear. Please forgive me for allowing rebelliousness to infiltrate my soul through my actions and thoughts.

I surrender every part of my soul that I have handed over to the enemy through my rebellious behavior. You, Jesus, are my Lord and Savior, and I willingly release control to You. I no longer seek to prove myself to others but place my complete trust in You, the God of hope. I give You my faith for the unseen, knowing that You are true and Your thoughts about me are the ones that truly matter.

I ask You to break every chain of bondage resulting from my rebelliousness, not only in my life but also in the lives of my children and future generations. Jesus, I invite Your Holy Spirit to fill every empty space in my soul that was once occupied by strongholds, replacing them with Your peace, the Shalom Peace.

I am deeply grateful, Lord Jesus, for what You have accomplished both on the Cross and in this very moment. Your blood holds ultimate authority over everything, and I celebrate the freedom You have graciously given me. I ask for Your strength, courage, and wisdom to resist partnering with rebellion, keeping my soul pure and reflecting Your image.

Thank You, Jesus, for Your everlasting love. Amen.

Chapter 14

Arise and Shine Ministries Deliverance Model

> *"And these signs will follow those who believe: In My name they will cast out demons; they will speak with new tongues; they will take up serpents; and if they drink anything deadly, it will by no means hurt them; they will lay hands on the sick, and they will recover."*
>
> Mark 16:17-18 NKJV

Deliverance is not reserved for those with deliverance ministries. Casting out demons is the right of every believer. Jesus demonstrated his love for others by healing the emotionally, physically oppressed and by casting out demons. The model of deliverance in this chapter is not the only model for deliverance: It is simply a guide to help you set the captives free. We are one of many methods and our model should always be used under the guidance of the Holy Spirit. Many other books have been written with deliverance models and guides. The Arise & Shine method is just one way to help set the captives free.

There are many things I wish I had known when I started in the deliverance ministry. Thankfully, there are some great ministries that teach others what to look for when you are getting started. For example, Pieter and I did not know that certain sexual spirits will almost always be present for someone who has been abused or molested. We learned the hard way and had to see a person more than once to get them totally free.

It is wisdom to seek training from someone who is actively moving in the deliverance ministry. Never be too proud to learn. Deliverance is humbling, yet so rewarding.

Dr. Rob Reimer has extensive experience in the deliverance ministry and has some phenomenal resources. He can be found at: www.renewalinternational.com . Dr. Rob Reimer's book, Soul Care, will help you on your soul healing journey.

There is simply nothing like seeing Jesus get his full reward when a captive is set free! I long to see a church walking in the freedom that Jesus died for. It is the church's great privilege to lead others to full freedom.

The deliverance model below is just one method. There are many ways to see the captives set free. I pray that you use this as a guide and follow the leading of the Holy Spirit above all other instructions. I bless you as you step into this exciting journey of seeing the captives set free!

General Guidelines for Deliverance

- The goal is to remove evil spirits that are present in the person's body or soul.
- The end goal is to lead people closer to Jesus - we want them to experience His love and to be filled with the Holy Spirit.
- Deliverance should only be ministered to believers (born-again Christians) or stronger demons can come back and fill the space where they left (See Matthew 12:45).
- Deliverance must be done in love and with dignity (See 1 Corinthians 13).
- Deliverance should be done with a team present, and one person should be responsible f or taking the lead (Ecclesiastes 4:12). The rest of the team should pray and report what they are sensing, if necessary.
- Deliverance leaders can switch places, but it can be confusing for the person if multiple people are asking questions and making commands.

- Speaking in an authoritative voice is necessary sometimes, but yelling at the person is never necessary.
- The person being ministered to should feel loved, covered, and safe (1 Corinthians 13).
- People of the opposite sex should have another person of that sex present in the room.
- Only get the information you need to get the person free - details of past events are not always necessary.
- Humility is required to minister deliverance. Deliverance means we get behind Jesus and the Holy Spirit, asking them what they want to do for this person.
- Be sure to let the person know they can stop the process anytime they start feeling unsafe.
- Believe that Jesus will show up and that He wants to set the person free! Faith is critical as ministers of deliverance. Faith is not a feeling, but a choice to trust the Lord as we minister freedom to others.

Open Doors That Can Give the Enemy Access To A Person's Life

- **Sexual Sin:** Sex or sexual acts outside of marriage will open a door.
- **Sexual Abuse:** We have never encountered an individual that was sexually molested who did not have demonic issues as a result. People who have been sexually abused, raped, or molested, should seek deliverance. Soul tie breaks are often necessary when sexual sin and abuse have occurred (See Chapter 9, Redeeming Purity and Sex in Marriage, for prayers to renounce sexual sin and to break soul ties).

- **Soul ties** should be broken with each sexual partner. Sexual abuse requires a soul tie break between the perpetrator and victim.
- **Sin:** Any sin mentioned in the Bible is an opening or access point: hate, long-term anger (more than one day), rage, jealousy, idolatry, hypocrisy, murder, abortion, etc..
- **Witchcraft:** We have never encountered a person who had engaged in witchcraft to not need some deliverance. This includes when the person's bloodline has engaged in witchcraft (See Chapter 10, Breaking free from Witchcraft and the Occult, for prayers for deliverance).
- **Rebellion:** Rebellion is the sin of witchcraft (1 Samuel 15:23). Jezebel is a prime example of control that manifested in witchcraft (see 1 Kings 21:7).
- **Lies and Vows:** Lies can give the enemy a foothold and give him an access point in our lives. Pay attention to lies a person believes as you minister deliverance. Lies and vows need to be repented for and renounced. (See Chapter 7, The Power of Forgiveness, for prayers to uncover the lies and vows in a person's life).
- **Fear:** Fear is an access point. Have the person repent for partnering with fear and renounce agreement with fear (see Romans 14:23).
- **Unforgiveness and Bitterness:** Unforgiveness and Bitterness is an access point for the enemy (See Chapter 7, The Power of Forgiveness, for prayers for deliverance).

Arise and Shine Ministries Deliverance Process

Step 1 - Preparing Yourself

Before the deliverance make sure you are totally free, and not living with any unconfessed sins. Demons will often call out sins that are unconfessed, and will attempt to embarrass the deliverance minister. Go into the session free and clear. Before the session, ask the Holy Spirit if there is anything that needs to be dealt with before you minister deliverance to another person. Be sure that you have gone through a thorough deliverance and inner healing process yourself before you attempt to set others free.

Step 2 - Pray, Fast, and Decree

Before you minister deliverance be sure that you have prayed for the person (if the deliverance was planned ahead of time). Fasting and prayer are powerful weapons against the enemy and his demons, although I have casted out many demons without fasting. Fasting is not a formula and should be Holy Spirit led. Decree total freedom over the person and his or her bloodline. Pray as the Holy Spirit prompts you to pray for the person. Be as specific as possible.

Step 3 - The Deliverance

Start by getting the life story from the person. Take time to write down key events in their lives. Getting the story will take time, but it is important not to skip this step. **Write down any of the "access points" mentioned above.** Have a tablet, computer, or notepad present to write down plenty of notes. Write everything down so that you can remember what spirits you still need to deal with.

Reporting

Be sure that the person knows they are supposed to report everything they feel, hear, sense, see, or know during the deliverance. The person's job is to tell you what they are experiencing, and this information will be vital during the process. Sometimes a specific event will come to the person's mind. It is important to pay attention to the details, because the event could be a clue as to what is happening (For example, if the individual thinks of an event involving the father or mother, the person could need to forgive the father or mother for that specific event. Pay attention to what the person tells you).

Making Decrees and Commands

The blood of Jesus is your most powerful weapon during deliverance. Demons hate the blood of Jesus. The more you talk about the blood, the weaker the demons become. Sometimes if demons are being stubborn, I will stop and worship and talk about the blood of Jesus and ask Angels to come assist. I will command the demons to look at the blood of Jesus, which they really hate.

Pray for the person and use the commands below to take authority over the demons in the person's life. Remember that as a believer, Jesus gave you authority to cast out demons (Luke 10:19).

- Pray how the Holy Spirit leads you.
- Decree: I decree total freedom for _____ in the name of Jesus.
- I pour the blood of Jesus over the ministry team and _____ (the name of the person you are ministering to).
- In the name of Jesus I command every spirit that left because they knew what we were doing today to be cut off from the person's life forever.
- In Jesus' name I cover the person with the blood of Jesus as well as all of the ministers in the room today.

- In Jesus' name I ask for angelic protection and assistance for our team and the person being ministered to.
- In the name of Jesus I command every spirit to line up in the center of the person's soul and stay in the hierarchy they are already in.
- I command the spirits to stay in the order they are already in.

Calling the spirits to attention

- **Goal:**
  1. Find out what demonic spirit is present. (ask what spirit the Lord Jesus wants to deal with - not what you think is present). Prophetic ministry is helpful, but we should ultimately hear from the person. Teach them not to pray during the ministry time, but just report what they are seeing, hearing, sensing, feeling, etc.
  2. What is the purpose or job of that spirit in the person's life?
  3. Does that spirit have a legal right to stay?
  4. Break agreement.
  5. Break the Curse of that spirit over the person's life.
  6. Finally, expel the spirit.
- **Step 1: Command:**
  - "First spirit that the Lord Jesus calls to attention; Come to the front and line up in the center of the person's soul." (We only want the spirit to come to the front that the Lord Jesus wants to deal with to come to the front first).
  - Command the spirit to tell you their name and their purpose in the person's life. If they won't give you this information, bind them and command them to step aside while you deal with the other spirits first.

- o **Ask / Command:** What is your purpose in the person's life?
- o **Ask / Command:** Do you (the demonic spirit) have any legal ground to stay in the person's life or any ground to come back?
- o **Ask / Command:** Is there another spirit you report to? Are there other spirits there with you who report to you?
  - The goal is to discover if they are working alone or in a hierarchy. Demons are rarely working alone. For example, Anger will often be with bitterness or rage). Although some of the weaker demons can be operating alone.
  - Write all the spirits down that are working together and bind them together.
- o **Ask / Command:** Are you a generational spirit? (Demons can enter a person through the unconfessed sins of their ancestors).
- o **Binding Lying or Blocking spirits:** Bind blocking or lying spirits that are giving you trouble. Command them to step aside to deal with them later.

- **Repent and Renounce:** It is critical that the individual you are ministering to says prayers out loud to break agreement with the spirits themselves. You are casting the demons out, but they must make a choice to be free. Have the person repeat the prayers below out loud as needed before you cast the spirit out. Sometimes there will be times that the spirit is acting so violently that you must act and take authority over that spirit for the person. This is definitely ok to do. Remember that you are in control and the Holy Spirit is there with you.)

- **Breaking Generational Curses:** Have the person repeat, "I repent for the sin of _____. Jesus, please forgive me and my ancestors for this sin. I renounce _____ (Say the name of the sin out loud, witchcraft, sexual sin, etc..). I cancel that sin and all of its effects on my life and the generations following me. I break the curse over my life and the life of my children."

- **Cancel the Curse:** Once you are sure the demon(s) do not have any legal right to come back, cancel the curse the demon brought over the person's life by saying: "spirit of anxiety and depression I cancel your curse over this person's life."

- **Cast Demons Out:** Cast out each demon by name. I find it best to cast out one at a time and to ask the person if they sense, see, or feel a release. The person will often know the demon has left. Do this until you encounter that the only spirit left is the Holy Spirit.

- **Stuck:** If you get stuck, take a break and seek the Lord in prayer. Try not to keep going if you really get stuck and can't get the person free. There is no shame in this happening. Ask the Lord if you should bring a more experienced person with you to help you finish the process. Seek the Lord to find out what is really happening with the person.

- **How do you know when the person is free?** Once there are no more demonic spirits present, the person will only sense the Holy Spirit's presence.

- **Finishing up:** Pray for the person to be filled with the Holy Spirit! This is a critical step!

Pray for the person and prophesy destiny and identity over the person. Ask the Holy Spirit to give the person a gift. Record this for the person if you can. We only want the person to remember what the Lord is saying about them.

Final Thoughts: Deliverance is meant to lead the person to Jesus. We want the person to see that Jesus did it all, and that He is the one who loves them, and that Jesus is the one protecting them. This should always be the goal as we minister to others. It is not about us and what we did, but rather what Jesus did.

Chapter 15

Follow up Care for Deliverance

"You will keep him in perfect peace, Whose mind is stayed on You, Because he trusts in You."

Isaiah 26:3 NKJV

Here are some of the steps for a believer to take post-deliverance:

- Continue to renew the mind through the word of God
- Find a church community
- Intimacy with the Father, Son and Holy Spirit

Mind Renewal through the Word of God

Renewing the mind is critical before and after inner healing and deliverance. Mind renewal will keep us centered on the truth of God's word, and will not allow space for the enemy to come back in and lie to us. Chapter four focuses on mind renewal, and the benefits of tearing down strongholds in our mind. Ministries such as Igniting Hope Ministries are helpful as they focus on the renewal of the mind.

After Pieter and myself were delivered, we still had many areas that needed sanctification. Although the demons were gone, we still needed to continue to renew our minds to the truth of God's Word. The journey of mind renewal is a daily transformation that takes place, causing us to see the truth from heaven's perspective. The good news is we are being transformed into the image of Christ! We can rest assured that He who began a good work in you will bring it to completion. The Lord moves us from glory to glory (see 2 Corinthians 3:18, Philippians 1:6).

Community

Finding a community of believers is important as you continue to learn and grow in the Lord. God simply did not design us to be alone. Jesus walked closely with the twelve disciples, and even closer with three of the disciples. Jesus demonstrated the importance of having others around to learn and grow in community.

One of the things the enemy loves to do is isolate us. When the prophet Elijah was feeling depressed, it was because he was alone and in a cave. He was ready to give up! This is a powerful picture of what happens when we go into a metaphorical "cave" and isolate ourselves from the body. Elijah needed encouragement, and he also needed food and rest or a "snack and a nap," as I like to say. He had no one present in his life to encourage him. Thankfully, the Lord sent an angel and food to give Elijah the encouragement and nourishment he so desperately needed.

Intimacy with Jesus, the Holy Spirit, and the Father

Intimacy is the reward of being sons and daughters of God. What good father would not want to spend time with his child? In the same way, we have a Father in heaven who longs to speak to us and spend time with us. The Father longs to connect with us, spirit to Spirit. Sometimes the process of learning to open your heart to God takes time.

There are many powerful resources and books available on developing intimacy, but the most important key is to connect with God in our secret place (see Psalm 91). The secret place is the place where we pray, worship, and take time to listen to our Father's voice. The secret place is not a location, but a heart posture. We are the secret place! He loves to be with us. The secret place is when we choose to connect with God, heart to heart. We put aside distractions and allow the love of God to fill us to overflowing.

Final Thoughts

Total freedom is possible through the blood of Jesus. He died so that we could live the abundant life! Do not settle for partial freedom. Pursue healing with all your heart and soul, and God will set you free. He truly is a good, good Father. I bless you in your healing journey as you discover true freedom through Jesus Christ. I bless you to know that you are a deeply loved, and cherished child of God. I pray that you know the love of Christ, which surpasses understanding.

More About Melinda & Pieter Lagaay

Pieter went to medical school and law school but fell into the bondage of pornography and sexual addiction. His professional career collapsed and they faced a likely second divorce. Then, simultaneously, Melinda heard the audible voice of God while Pieter had an open vision and encountered Jesus.

Today Pieter and Melinda's marriage is stronger than it has ever been. It is filled with a deep love because they have seen the wounds of each other's hearts healed. Melinda and Pieter are passionate about seeing marriages restored and thriving.

Pieter and Melinda moved to Northern California in 2020 to attend ministry school at Bethel School of Supernatural Ministry. Pieter is the founder of Bezalel Innovations and Melinda is the Beliefs Training Director at Igniting Hope Ministries. Pieter and Melinda co-founded Arise & Shine Ministries, which focuses on Inner Healing and Deliverance.

Melinda and Pieter live in Palo Cedro, California on a mini-farm, and attend Bethel Church in Redding, California. They have three adult children, two dogs, four cats, several goats, and chickens.

Arise & Shine Ministries www.ariseandshinetoday.com

Bezalel Innovations www.bezalelinnovations.com

Made in the USA
Coppell, TX
17 February 2026

72281960R00087